Afro-Brazilians in Telenovelas

Afro-Brazilians in Telenovelas

Social, Political, and Economic Realities

Samantha Nogueira Joyce

LEXINGTON BOOKS
Lanham • Boulder • New York • London

Published by Lexington Books
An imprint of The Rowman & Littlefield Publishing Group, Inc.
4501 Forbes Boulevard, Suite 200, Lanham, Maryland 20706
www.rowman.com

86-90 Paul Street, London EC2A 4NE

British Library Cataloguing in Publication Information Available

Library of Congress Cataloging-in-Publication Data Available

ISBN: 978-1-7936-4423-7 (cloth)
ISBN: 978-1-7936-4424-4 (electronic)
ISBN: 978-1-7936-4425-1 (pbk.)

To Mike, Tabatha, and Wyatt.

Contents

Acknowledgments

The first draft of this manuscript was written during extremely trying times: the COVID-19 lockdown and the months that followed. With this in mind, I would like to thank God, and everyone who helped me along the way, weather emotionally: Mike, Tabatha, and Wyatt Joyce; academically, by reading early drafts and providing support: Denise Witzig and Myrna Santiago; by helping with formatting and creating a reference list: Julia Oliveira; by letting me borrow a book or two: Julie Reiss; or by keeping my body moving through capoeira and giving my brain much needed relief: Uriel Arauz, Armando Baqueta Ibarra, Faith Bruxa Hoenecke, Kelly Guerreira Schumann, Rose Fininha Gear, Mestre Ganso Sabiá, and Anna Batida Chock. Obrigada!

Introduction
What (Racial) Democracy?

In 2018 the Brazilian telenovela *Segundo Sol* ("Second Sun") aired over the course of six months. The show was set in the coastal state of Bahia, where the majority of the population of approximately 15 million people is either Black or mestizo. Yet of the show's 27 actors, only 3 were Black, and none of them played a major role, or even appeared in the first episode (Cowie 2018, para 6). This imbalance is notable in and of itself, but is particularly significant since the telenovela aired during the anniversary year of two watersheds for racial progress in Brazil. First, 2018 marked the 130th anniversary of the Brazilian Golden Law (*Lei Áurea*), which abolished slavery in the country and freed all those who were held in captivity. The law was signed by Princess Isabel, then exercising regency in the imperial government of Brazil, during the absence of her father, Emperor D. Pedro II. Second, *Segundo Sol* came ten years after TV Globo aired *Duas Caras* ("Two Face") (2008), the first Brazilian telenovela with an Afro-Brazilian actor as its protagonist, and the first in which the writer/director, through his personal blog, maintained a direct dialogue with the public about the racism represented in the plot, as well as in Brazilian society more broadly.

This book offers a textual comparative analysis between *Segundo Sol* and *Duas Caras*. In so doing, it reaffirms the importance of the telenovela genre as a major site of debate and identity negotiation related to the persistent racism in Brazilian TV specifically, and in Brazilian society more generally. Throughout, the book also traces historical and cultural similarities related to attitudes toward race between Brazil and the United States, such as the rise of populist conservativism in both countries (i.e., the elections of Jair Bolsonaro in 2018 and Donald Trump in 2016), as well as similarities in the depiction of Blacks in Brazilian and American media. Overall, the book shows that telenovelas are still a powerful agent/catalyst for social change in Brazil,

1

especially those regarding racial relations and changes in attitude toward racism. This analysis also examines how racial change in Brazil plays out in discussions within the telenovela (plot, dialogues, and so on) and debates about the telenovelas (several media outlets, interpersonal dialogue, etc.).

Therefore, this book is a part of a research continuum about telenovelas and identity that builds upon a broad global research agenda, but more specifically, extends and adds to the book *Brazilian Telenovelas and the Myth of Racial Democracy* (2012). The two books are similar in methodology (open textual analysis) but also differ in many ways. Whereas in my previous book I examined what happened when a telenovela intentionally and directly addressed matters of race and racism in Brazil (from inception) in order to challenge race and the Myth of Racial Democracy, at that time, the current analysis focuses, amongst other things on the power of social media activism to actually change a telenovela that did not set out to address race at all. The current research also discusses how the myth has been perpetuated at times, and sometimes challenged. Additionally, akin to the previous examination, this current analysis focuses on the complicated terrain in which the telenovela text navigates; one that is tied to socio, economical, and political factors in the Brazilian society, exploring the ways in which telenovelas function as a two-way mirror reflecting and challenging current and/or ingrained trends, beliefs, and ideologies.

Thus, while many in the media, the Black Movement, and academia have argued that the traditional notion of Brazil as a "racial democracy"—or the idea that Brazil has escaped racial discrimination due to its history of miscegenation no longer exists, as discussed in *Brazilian Telenovelas and the Myth of Racial Democracy* (2012), it is important to recognize that the term "racial democracy" and its meaning remain contested, and many in Brazil still view the country as racially egalitarian. Indeed, while the Black and Brown Brazilian population who experience social and institutional racism may laugh at the concept, the idea of a utopian racial paradise was heavily used from 2007 to 2016 when the country was bidding for, preparing for, and eventually hosting the Summer Olympics. For example, in making Brazil's bid, then-president Luiz Inácio Lula da Silva (Lula) evoked the trope of racial unity with none other than Pelé, the internationally renowned Black soccer player, at his side, which leant credibility to the Lula's assertion that Brazilians are racially united and proud of it. As Lula stated at the time of the bid,

With great pride, I represent here the hopes and dreams of more than 190 million Brazilians. We are a people passionate about sports. Looking at the five Olympic rings, I see my country in them. We are not only a mixed people, but a people who love to be mixed (Maranhão, 2009, para 11).

Such discourse casting Brazil as a racial utopia is rooted in the Racial Democracy ideology, which is tied to the idea of *branqueamento*—or "whitening" through miscegenation. Branqueamento is a mythological construct that works well as a political discourse that sells Brazil as free of racism, when in fact Black, Brown, and mixed Brazilians suffer institutionalized as well as socialized racism every day. The Racial Democracy ideology also has its roots in the teachings of Brazilian anthropologist Gilberto Freyre (1933–1983), one of its most prominent defenders. Freyre used Brazil's history of white-European colonization and miscegenation with Indigenous peoples and enslaved Africans to back up his claims. Thus, the core of the Racial Democracy ideology—whitening—reveals that it is in itself a racist construct.

So, it is imperative to take a historical look at race in order to unveil the myth of whitening through miscegenation (*branqueamento*) at the heart of the Brazilian ideology of racial democracy. This concept of race is clearly distinct from the dominant ideologies of race in the United States. For example, while in the United States for most purposes a binary code is used—you are either Black or white, in much of Latin America, the code that dominates is one which values you by how close to white you appear. It is assumed that the closer you are to the "white" side of the scale, the more beautiful, intelligent, and respected you are. Consequently, the very concept of whitening is at the heart of Brazil's discourse of racial democracy, revealing its racist nature from its inception (Joyce, 2012, p.24).

The idea of Brazil as a racial democracy has had a lasting social and legal legacy in the country. For example, in contrast to the United States, in Brazil there has been no race-based barriers to legal equality: there was no equivalent to the United States' "separate but equal law" in Brazil. For many years, there were also no affirmative action policies in Brazil, such as quotas, or any antidiscrimination laws. Quite simply, an ideology of Racial Democracy meant there was no need for race-based legal protections.[1] However, while racism remains, such laws (such as racial quotas) are now in place and were implemented when TV Globo announced its mostly white cast, as we will see in the sections bellow.

METHODOLOGY

As briefly mentioned above, the methodology used in this research is similar to that I employed in *Brazilian Telenovelas and the Myth of Racial Democracy*. Most saliently, I draw from the British and Latin American Cultural Studies traditions, which have focused on the relationship between the people, state, and the media, and how to construct truly democratic media within largely free-market economies. As García Canclini (2001) demonstrates, this requires an examination of the audiences' uses of mediated messages, the organizations of civil society, and the increasingly autonomous, powerful, and transnational media and culture industries. Latin American cultural scholars add to a body of research that concerns itself with a quest for communication theories of and for democratic practice, and the creation of multiple voices and public spheres, such as the one I present in this comparative study.

Because no text stands on its own, apart from its social, political, and economic milieu, my investigation also includes looking at the zeitgeist in which *Segundo Sol* and *Duas Caras* were produced and consumed in order to bring scholarly insight into the cultural, political, and economic significance of the telenovela genre. Thus, I am examining how the findings are connected to larger social and historical issues. I start my analysis by looking at the racial landscape in Brazil from an historical perspective, followed by an examination of racial representations in Brazilian telenovelas today, including what they say about the country socially, politically, and economically. I then delve into the methodology used which borrows from British and Latin American traditions, adding that if Stuart Hall recognized audiences as active, due to technological advances and changes in connectivity, we can also consider them activists. Finally, I offer a comparative textual examination between the characters of *Segundo Sol* and *Duas Caras*, tracing lingering stereotypes while discussing the possibilities and limitations that affect such representation.

Additionally, theoretically, this research considers telenovelas to be "agenda setters." In this, it is akin to Joyce & Martinez's (2016) work, in the sense that I understand telenovelas to function not only as a site of struggle for meaning and identities, but also as "news medium, in other words, one that presents the public with current events and functions as an aggregator and curator of newsworthy elements" (p. 79). When I refer to "text" in this book, I take a semiotician perspective akin to Roland Barthes' by critically analyzing the "text" beyond dialogue or spoken/written words: my analysis includes production elements such as choice of actors, story line, costuming, camera angles, ideological values, connotations, myths, assumptions, as well as the programming time slot my objects of study occupied on the daily television grid-prime time.

SEGUNDO SOL

Segundo Sol (SS) debuted on May 14, 2018. It aired on TV Globo's, during the at 9pm[2] timeslot (traditional prime time). Set in the state of Bahia, the show starts in 1999 and then takes a leap 20 years into the future (to 2018). On the surface, the main plot of the program is fantastical and akin to most of its kind: it revolves around Beto Falcão, a once famous (white) singer from Bahia who is on the verge of irrelevance and who is on his way to a performance at a different city when he misses his flight. However, the plane he was supposed to be on crashes, and he is presumed dead. Pressured by his fiancée and brother to cash in on his "posthumous" fame to help his struggling family, Falcão takes on another identity, as Miguel. He then takes refuge on a largely somewhat deserted island, where he falls in love with Luzia, a mother of two who was wrongly accused of assassinating her husband and forced to flee the country. To protect herself, Luzia likewise assumed a new, fictional identity. Luzia comes back 20 years later as an accomplished DJ, and with a new name (Ariela), to reclaim her innocence, family, and Miguel.

Though the plot itself is fantastical and entertaining, *Segundo Sol* also has a much more serious function as a social commentary. Most significantly, it helps reveal a lingering racism in Brazil, illustrating how racial democracy is a myth more than a reality and reasserting the program's role in highlighting and igniting this debate (Araújo, 2000; Joyce, 2012). For example, *Segundo Sol* was set in Bahia, the Brazilian state with the highest concentration, and where 76 percent of the population declared themselves Black or Brown on the latest census. Yet when TV Globo released the initial promotional clip for the show, only 3 of the 27 actors' whose names appeared were Black, and only one received airtime. Moreover, of the 35 actors who appeared over the course of the program, only five were Black. This scarcity of Black actors produced a strong reaction from viewers on social media, as well as garnered the attention of the national and international press. In that first promo, of the 27 actors' names on the clip, only 3 were Black and only one was shown visually on the screen received airtime. Thus, it is no surprise that the promo was received with harsh criticism and inspired a viral Internet campaign— *#EuPoderiaEstarEmSegundoSol* ("I could be in *Second Sun*"). The campaign offered suggestions of several Black actors who could have been part of the program with the accompanying hashtag (Terto, 2018; Barros, 2018b). In light of such criticism related to the apparent racism in the casting, TV Globo announced that,

> The criteria for casting a telenovela are technical and artistic. Globo does not base these decisions on the skin color of actors, but on the suitability to the character profile, talent, and availability of the cast. We believe that this is the most correct way to do it. A story like *Segundo Sol*, due to the fact that it takes place in Bahia, brings us many opportunities undoubtedly to reflect on diversity issues in society, which will be addressed throughout the telenovela, which is structured in two phases. The manifestations of criticism we have seen so far

are based mainly on the release of the first phase of the program, which focuses on the plot that sets up the rest of the series. We are attentive, listening, and following these comments, confident that we still have a lot of stories to tell ahead of us! (Tert, 2018, para 14)

TV Globo's response was not received well, as it seemed to imply that Black actors were either not talented enough for the show, and/or that TV Globo did not have enough available actors of African descent on its payroll. Within days, the response lead to a group of TV Globo actors of African descent to immediately confront the network and to publicly question the lack of Black professionals in telenovelas, especially in one set in Bahia. The network replied that they recognized that they currently have a "less representation than what we would like," showing more awareness than they did earlier that week with the initial statement (Atores da Globo, 2018, para 4).

In order to understand the nature and extent of the shockwaves created by the mere promo of an upcoming program, we must first understand Brazil's racial history, as well as the social, political, and economic roles of telenovelas in Brazil. I discuss these themes below.

CONTEXTUALIZING RACE IN BRAZIL

In 1888, Brazil became the last country in the Americas to abolish slavery, over 350 years after the first Africans were brought to the then-Portuguese colony as enslaved people. When Princess Isabel signed the Golden Law (Lei Áurea) on May 13, it was almost an inevitability that slavery would legally end, since all other countries had ended the institution and a great portion of Brazilian slaves had emancipated themselves by starting their runaway slave communities, called *quilombos*.

Though slavery was illegal for the whole of the twentieth century, the issue of race was prominent throughout Brazilian society, and remains so today. In Brazil, the way in which the concept of race is socially constructed differs drastically from the binary racial discourse in the United States. In Brazil, widespread miscegenation, or the mixing of races, during the era of slavery and beyond lead to an understanding that a person's race depends mainly on their phenotype (i.e., how they appear). Race is not defined directly by genetics or by blood; and in contrast to America, there was never anything resembling the "one drop rule" in Brazil. As Daniel (2006) states, racial blending in Brazil gave rise to a ternary racial project, not a binary one, which differentiates the population into *brancos* (whites), *Pardos* (multiracial individuals, also popularly known as *mulatos*), and *Pretos* (Blacks) (p. xi). Thus, "on paper," discourse of miscegenation seemed like a good idea, as Araújo (2008) explains:

> The affirmation of miscegenation was always associated with the idea that on this land a nation was created with a new race. Brazilians, fruit of a hybridism where racial and cultural homogeneity would prevail, would leave behind, and overcome in a new way, the racial division of our formation. In this context, the well-known myth of Brazilian racial democracy is born (p. 982).

However, while abolitionists and others used the discourse of miscegenation as a way to avoid race polarization in Brazil (Santos, 2002), the concept of miscegenation still had its origins in racist ideologies, such as *branqueamento*, or "whitening," and in the Brazilian miscegenation and whitening discourse, it is widely assumed that the closer you are to the "white" side of the scale, the more beautiful, intelligent, and respected you are. And this overall assumption seems to hold true both in real life and in the "imagined" one, on the television screen. Thus, we can conclude that: the concept of whitening is at the core of Brazil's discourse of racial democracy, revealing its racist nature from its foundation (Joyce, 2012, p. 24).

Importantly, the legacy of slavery in Brazil is also manifest in lingering class differences, lack of opportunity and social mobility, and the perpetuation of a cycle of poverty and violence among large segments of the population. According to the United Nations website, seven out of ten people murdered in Brazil are Black. In the 15–29 age group, five Black lives are lost to violence every two hours. And from 2005 to 2015, while the homicide rate per 100,000 inhabitants fell by 12 percent for non-Blacks, among Blacks there was an increase of 18.2 percent. Additionally, the United Nations reports that 56 percent of Brazilians agree with the statement that the violent death of a Black youth is less disturbing than the death of a white youth. And, according to the United Nations Children's Fund (UNICEF), four out of every thousand Brazilian teenagers will be assassinated before turning 19; this means 43,000 Brazilians between the ages of 12 and 18 from 2015 to 2021, three times more Blacks than whites (Pelo Fim, para 3–7). Economically, Blacks occupy only 4.7 per cent of executive posts in the country's top 500 companies, while Black workers are paid about 40 per cent less than their white counterparts. Blacks also comprise only about 20 per cent of Brazil's lower house of congress (Leahy & Scipany, 2018, para 12).

Although whitening as an ideology is no longer explicitly disseminated, TV Globo telenovelas continue to be largely monochromatic in terms of their casts, and do not reflect the multiracial nature of Brazilian society. Yet, while this discrepancy between the social reality and what is depicted on the television screen may have gone largely unquestioned in previous generations, television viewing habits have changed with the advancement of the internet. Today, viewers are much less passive than they were in the past: they make themselves heard online, loud and clear, prompting traditional media giants such as TV Globo to respond and change their course of action, as exemplified by the "I Could Be in Second Sun" campaign.

A BRIEF HISTORY OF TV GLOBO

Although television first appeared in Brazil in 1950, with the now extinct network Rede Tupi, the Brazilian giant Rede Globo did not launch until 1965, born out of a joint venture with Time-Life in 1964. However, a mere four years after its inception, the military government intervened to expel Time-Life in a strategic move toward market concentration, which was connected with the military's obsession with national integration (Rêgo, 2009, pp. 38–44).

Yet the dismantling of the joint venture did not hurt TV Globo. In fact, it actually aided the network since several employees who originally came from Time-Life elected to stay with Globo, which helped the company establish itself as an extremely efficient U.S.-style network administration, giving it an edge over other Brazilian channels (Straubhaar, 1991, pp. 47–48). Thus, TV Globo as a media success story was historically closely linked to its access to state-of-the-art technology and know-how, as well as to its cozy relationship with the government during the military dictatorship in the 1960s. More recently, its success can also be attributed to high investment in pre/postproduction and an increased reliance on transmedia storytelling, which has changed how television programming, and more specifically Brazilian telenovelas, are being produced and consumed (Joyce, 2020, p. 1).

While it may seem unexpected that TV Globo's enduring success is reliant on a traditional form of television storytelling, telenovelas have been the highest rated program in Brazil for over sixty years; Brazil remains one of the Latin American countries where telenovelas still dominate the daily TV schedules. Thus, it is no surprise that TV Globo—the country's largest media conglomerate—is working hard to keep the classic format vital by ensuring that its programming has a look and feel that modern audiences expect (Joyce, 2020, pp. 10–11).

Finally, being up-to-date aesthetically and thematically in terms of its programming help insure that the business and economic sides of the media conglomerate are alive and well. For example, while research shows that Brazil has followed the global trend of audience stratification due to advances in technology (streaming services such as Netflix, for example), the traditional telenovela genre is still the number one locally produced and consumed program in the country, able to attract 100 million viewers a day, which is about half of the country's population. This massive popularity makes telenovelas, especially popular ones on TV Globo, highly attractive to advertisers (Kaiser, 2019, p. 20).

TV GLOBO AND THE REPRESENTATION OF RACE

Brazilian telenovelas, as Martín-Barbero (2001) reminds us, are extremely complex: more than melodramatic commercial narratives, telenovelas are a cultural phenomenon through which people constitute and reconstitute their identities. They are a site of mediations, a space for struggle of signification, and a powerful vehicle for stimulating knowledge, discourse, and discussion in the social production of meaning (Martín-Barbero, 1993). Put another way, telenovelas are a site of negotiation and creation of identity, a place for "struggle for signification that goes beyond a marketplace; a space that can activate dialogue in the social production of meaning" (Joyce, 2012, p. 46). Indeed, even while reproducing racial stereotypes, telenovela's place of importance in Latin American society is such that it opens up alternative spaces of dialogue about race and racism in mediums such as blogs, news programs, specialized outlets, and social media. As exemplified by the reaction to the promo video of *Segundo Sol*, debate sometimes begins even before a program actually airs. As previously noted, the 9 o'clock telenovela spot, is still the number one rated program in Brazil, highlighting not only its sociopolitical importance, but its economic prominence as well.

And this economic role is not merely a national one: TV Globo telenovelas have been a staple of Brazilian TV since its inception and a lucrative export for the network, operating on a transnational space, being imported by over 140 countries (Joyce & La Pastina, 2017). For a decade, the top ten rated shows in Brazil were not only telenovelas, but were all TV Globo productions. According to the Ibero American Observatory of Television, which monitors television viewership in twelve countries,[3] TV Globo's productions have also consistently taken the number one spot in each of those countries (Lopes & Gómez, 2017, pp. 114–125).

Because of their cultural, social, and economic significance, telenovelas have received much interest from scholars over the years. Investigating the representation of social groups in telenovelas, for example, has been an important and recurring topic of academic research. Data produced by researchers interested in this topic shows that racial stereotypes and/or the lack of representational racial diversity have been a persistent modus operandi by TV Globo productions for decades. For example, Candido, Campos & Feres (2014) investigated 101 telenovelas from 1995–2014, and concluded that on average, 90 percent of characters in TV Globo telenovelas are represented by white actors/actresses, and only 10 percent by Black or Browns actors/actresses. Such scenario does not match the diversity of the national reality, which states that the Brazilian population of Blacks and browns exceeds that of whites, according to the Brazilian Institute of Geography and Statistics (IBGE). That percentage has varied very little in the last twenty years, despite localized efforts to produce soap operas with greater participation of Blacks (Candido, Campos & Feres, 2014, para 3). It is also noteworthy that until the end of the 1990s the number of Black actors hired by TV Globo only slightly exceeded 10 percent of the network's total cast. Consequently, as Araújo (2008) states, in a country that has a population of about 50 percent of afro-descendants, "this is a striking demonstration that the telenovela has never respected the ethnic-racial definitions that Brazilians make of themselves" (p. 979). Indeed, such an imbalance in such an influential cultural product as the TV Globo telenovela highlights how Brazil's racial democracy is a myth more than a reality, one that claims that "due to our condition as a mestizo nation we overcame the 'racial problem' and we are a model of integration for the world" (Araújo, 2008, p. 979).

Investigating Black representation, and the lack thereof, in such influential and transnational products such as telenovelas is important for a number of reasons. As Araújo (2008) suggests that,

> by not giving visibility to the true racial composition of the country, the telenovela conservatively agrees with the use of miscegenation as a shield to avoid recognition of the importance of the Black population in Brazilian history and cultural life. It agrees with an imagery of servitude and inferiority of Black people in Brazilian society—thus participating in a massacre against what should be seen as our greatest cultural heritage in the face of a world divided by sectarianisms and ethnic and religious wars—the pride of our multiraciality (p. 982).

As discussed in *Brazilian Telenovelas and the Myth of Racial Democracy*, some key aspects regarding how Afro-Brazilians are represented in telenovelas at times have to do with the writer's personal agendas but definitely reflect and sometimes challenge the cultural, political, socioeconomic zeitgeist of the time of production. I will address these themes below.

BRAZIL THEN AND NOW

A lot has changed in the Brazilian landscape since *Duas Caras* aired in 2008. At that time, Brazilians were experiencing an era of progressive politics. For example, in 2010 Dilma Rousseff, of President Lula's Workers' Party, became Brazil's first female president. Rousseff sought to implement a progressive government agenda that focused on class and racial mobility, and on remedying Brazil's legacy of slavery and poverty. A year later, Rousseff's government launched *Brasil Sem Miséria* / "Brazil without Poverty" (2011), a welfare program aimed at lifting millions out of extreme poverty. In 2012, Parliament approved an affirmative action law for universities that required them to reserve 50 percent of their admissions for students from state-funded schools (who are traditionally lower class and non-white), as well as to increase the number of spaces allotted to Black, mixed-race, and Indigenous students. Furthermore, Brazilian Afro-heritage took a global center stage in in 2014, when UNESCO added Capoeira, the Afro-Brazilian art of resistance that mixes dance and a deadly martial art and was first used by enslaved people as a survival and self-emancipation technique and was inscribed on its List of the Intangible Cultural Heritage of Humanity (Brazil Profile, 2019, para 39–45).

The political climate in Brazil started to take a turn when in 2015, a year after Dilma Rousseff had been reelected president, Petrobras, the state oil company, was implicated in a massive corruption scandal. The scandal brought hundreds of thousands of protestors into the streets against President Rousseff, who had been the company's chairperson during the period in question. In 2018, senators voted to remove her from office for illegally using money from state banks to bankroll public spending. In October of that year, Brazilians elected far-right candidate Jair Bolsonaro, popularly known as "Trump of the Tropics," as president (Brazil Profile, 2019, para 47–49).

Thus, when *Segundo Sol* began airing in 2018, it did so against a backdrop of political and social turmoil in Brazil. President Bolsonaro, elected with 55 percent of the popular vote, quickly became known for freely making bigoted, misogynistic, and racially insensitive remarks, such as "(Brazilian) Indians are undoubtedly changing. . . . They are increasingly becoming human beings just like us" (Phillips, 2020, para 2). Bolsonaro has also insulted Black descendants of rebel African slaves called *quilombolas* and expressed regret about their legal protections. He has strongly hinted that one of his policy targets is Brazil's affirmative action program (Phillips, 2020, para 2).

Between the early1500s and the middle of the nineteenth century, Brazil had an estimated 5.5 million Africans brought to the country, compared with 500,000 transported to the United States. Today, Afro-Brazilians and those of mixed race constitute 76 percent of the bottom tenth of income earners, and receive the poorest quality education in the country. However, Bolsonaro does not see a link between slavery and the lingering racial and class divide, and has stated: "What debt to slavery? I never enslaved anyone in my life. Look, if you really look at history, the Portuguese didn't even step foot in

Africa. The Blacks themselves turned over the slaves" (Brazil's New Racist President, 2018, para 5–7).

Despite Bolsonaro's assertions to the contrary, slavery has left a mark in Brazil not only in terms of racial inequities, but also as an economic chiasm: Afro-descendants, who accounted for 55 percent of Brazil's population of 205.5 million in 2016, were about 50 percent more likely to be unemployed than whites, according to figures from the country's statistics bureau. Additionally, widespread violence involving Blacks was highlighted by their disproportionately being killed by police officers—in 2018 of Marielle Franco, a Black Rio de Janeiro city council woman and an outspoken critic of police violence in the slums: "This reality is contrary to Brazil's self-image as a rainbow society, a narrative that dates to the 1930s when Brazilian sociologist Gilberto Freyre argued that Brazil's mixed breeding between white masters and Black slaves produced a sort of ethnic democracy" (Leahy & Scipany, 2018, para 8–12).

As discussed above, television, and more specifically telenovelas, offers a site of struggle over competing ideologies: for example, the myth of racial democracy, and the reaction to the *Segundo Sol* promo lacking Black Brazilians and the subsequent campaign created by online activists. The attention garnered by the campaign, TV Globo's lack of Black representation, and the attention it received in the national and international media prompted the Ministério Público do Trabalho/ Public Ministry of Labor (MPT), through the national coordinator for the promotion of equality of opportunity and the elimination of discrimination in the workplace (*Coordigualdade*), to send TV Globo a recommendation as far as the representation and lack of representation of Blacks in its upcoming production. The MPT stated that the non-mirroring of society in television programs perpetuates anti-Black stereotypes and reaffirms the exclusion of spaces to be occupied by Blacks (Travae 2018b, para 8).

The Statute of Racial Equality recommends the MPT to promote actions that ensure equal opportunities in the labor market for the Black population, including the implementation of measures aimed at promoting equality in hiring in the public sector, and encouraging the adoption of similar measures in private businesses and organizations. According to the national coordinator of *Coordigualdade*, Valdirene Silva de Assis, "We decided to send this note, in order to show the company the importance of complying with laws addressing racial diversity. Despite being an artistic work and an open work, we believe that the program [*Segundo Sol*] has an obligation to include Black actors in sufficient proportion for a real representation of society" (Travae 2018b, para 9–10).

TV Globo responded by claiming that the issues regarding the lack of Black actors would be resolved in the second "phase" of the telenovela. However, as I discuss below, stereotypical representations remained.

SEGUNDO SOL AND DUAS CARAS

Persisting stereotypes of Blacks such as being poor, zealous maids, service workers, hyper sexualized, and classless, or, as in the case of Black women, Jezebels, as Boylorn (2008) calls them, can be identified as representational tropes in both programs currently being analyzed. And unfortunately, such representational tropes can be identified in both programs currently being analyzed. While *Duas Caras* seemed to reflect a progressive moment in Brazilian TV with its complex and multi layered Black protagonist Evilásio, what we see with *Segundo Sol* is a result of what Santos (2013) calls institutional racism, or those strategies and mechanisms that prevent the access of parts of the population to places of privilege and power, in this case of Blacks to the number one program in Brazilian television. One consequence of this lack of diversity is the reliance on stereotypes when groups without power appear in such representational spaces.

In everyday life, institutional racism ensures the maintenance of relationships of domination and oppression, becoming naturalized in countries such as Brazil, even with its high levels of miscegenation. In Brazil, institutional racism is manifest as "Racismo à la brasileira" (Brazilian Racism), which differs from the institutionalized racism of the United States, with its segregation laws, or South Africa, which had apartheid. According to Kabengele Munanga, a Congolese professor of anthropology at the University of São Paulo, in Brazil, it is the extremely problematic de facto racism: "It is not openly admitted, there is no law . . . therefore, it is difficult to fight" (Leahy & Scipany, 2018, para 13–14).

While there is a clear general parallel of stereotypical representations in *Duas Caras* and *Segundo Sol*, it is important to note that such stereotypes are not exclusive to Brazilian telenovelas. In fact, a parallel has been traced to the historical stereotypical representation of American Blacks in visual productions—classified by Bogle (2001) as "Toms," "Coons," "Mullattoes," "Mammies," and "Bucks"—sharing similarities with the representation of Blacks in Brazilian telenovelas (Bogle, 2001; Joyce, 2012). Such stereotypes were present to a certain extent in *Duas Caras*, despite its protagonist being a just and honest Black man, and were particularly prominent in *Segundo Sol*, as I will demonstrate in the textual analysis below.

It is important to mention that this type of analysis understands the text not as mathematical data, but as a means by which we study a signification process, a representation of reality; therefore, it is one that is worthy of attention. While I understand that telenovelas are a commercial program made for profit, I am also following the Latin American Cultural Studies tradition, which stresses the need to go beyond the manipulative and commercial role of the media.[4] We cannot disregard the fact that people look more and more to commercial media offerings than to abstract rules of democracy due to a discredit in political organizations. In this scenario, "consumption can be a site of cognitive value, it can be good for thinking and acting in a meaningful way that renews social life" (García Canclini 2001, pp. 5 & 47).

OUTLINE OF CHAPTERS

Following this introduction, in Chapter 1, "From Active to Active-ism," I continue to trace the history and the social, economic, and political roles played by Brazilian telenovelas by situating them within the Cultural Studies Tradition. I then discuss the changes in audience viewership and how viewers participate in not only the reading of the text, but in the production as well as consumption of telenovelas. Concepts such as the "open text" and Brazilians' persistent desire for the traditional television set as a mode of viewership are also examined. Further, the chapter looks at how advancements in technology have allowed the audience to not just be active viewers, but to in fact be activists (using the pun "active-ists") and cowriters of discourses and meanings, for example, those surrounding race and racism in Brazil.

In Chapter 2 "Her Body: From Baby Mamma to Mammie," I identify a persistent stereotype present in *Segundo Sol* that builds on a caricature of the older Black woman which Bogle described as "Mammie." In broad terms, "Mammie" is the mature, kind, usually heavy-set Black female who takes care of a white family as her own and may in fact be considered a fixture of the household, albeit a non-white one. While the protagonists and the majority of actors in *Segundo Sol* were white, we can clearly pinpoint who the Black leading actors are: Not only because there were few Black actors, but also because they are the ones with spoken lines, recurring appearances, and due to the fact that their actions are influenced or influence those of other leading characters.

Zefa is the mother of another character in telenovela: Roberval. Interestingly enough while Zefa is kind, passive and even submissive, especially to her white bosses, Roberval has the traditional characteristics of a villain in the narrative. In any case, Zefa's story line as Mammie goes as follows: she is the older, Black housekeeper who gave her white skinned son to her white employers to raise as their own but kept her Black-skinned son to herself. Key to this storyline is the fact that her white employer Severo fathered both of her kids (one phenotypically white, the other Black). When the family secret is revealed, a series of powerful dialogues between mother and son question the Brazilian racial discourse as well as Zefa's subservient position to her twenty-first-century "masters," a reference to slavery. As in the previous research *Brazilian Telenovelas and the Myth of Racial Democracy*, the fictional racial discourse surrounding these issues are key to help us understand the lingering discourses of race, racism, and the construction of Brazilian Black identity as well as those issues surrounding the racial democracy myth in Brazil.

Chapter 3, "His Body: Slaves, Bucks, Villains, and N*gg@s" examines the representation of two Black male characters in *Segundo Sol*. The first is Roberval, a neglected son in search of revenge against his white father Severo, who abandoned him but raised his lighter-skinned brother. The second is Acácio, a poor young Black man who is dating the white adopted daughter of none other than Severo. Acácio's storyline in *Segundo Sol* reminds us of Evilásio's plotline in *Duas Caras*, in which the Black protagonist who lived in a *favela* (a shanty town) in the outskirts or Rio and was the romantic interest for the white rich protagonist Júlia. In *Segundo Sol*, Acácio has all the former characteristics represented by Evilásio, but instead of living in a *favela* in Rio de Janeiro he lives in an illegally occupied house in Salvador. This chapter looks at how the clash between rich and poor, Black and white, educated and non-educated played out in similar ways in the two telenovelas, as well as the persistence of a lingering representational stereotype: the sexually insatiable Black man who lusts after white women, or what Bogle described as a "Buck."

It is important to note that not only are all three Black characters portrayed several times in bed with various white women; moreover, Acácio is seen having a taboo threesome with two mixed race girls. And minutes later, in a follow up scene ("after sex"), he is shown in bed, under sheets with them, having a conversation about his love for his white girlfriend. Key to the analysis of these characters is the multilayered aspects of the "text": dialogue, storyline, production elements such as editing, camera angles and clothing—or lack of clothing and how, taken together, they help us to understand what the program presents as what it means to be a Black man in Brazil.

In Chapter 4, "Blackness beyond Black Bodies: Candomblé and Capoeira," I examine the representation of two staples of Afro-Brazilian culture, heritage, and syncretism: Candomblé and Capoeira. Candomblé is an Afro-Brazilian religion that combines elements of Yoruba, Bantu, and Catholicism, and was developed in Bahia by enslaved Africans. In *Segundo Sol*, Pai Didico (Father Didico) is looking for a successor to lead his terreiro (temple). A similar storyline was present in *Duas Caras* with Mãe Setembrina passing away and with Andréia Biju taking the role as the new leader of the *terreiro*. While the recurrence of a story line about the underrepresented Afro-Brazilian religion may seem progressive, this chapter shows that in *Segundo Sol* the Afro-religion was associated with evil deeds, such as the killing of a white character. Capoeira is the deadly Afro-Brazilian martial art that combines elements of fight, acrobatics, music, dance, and rituals developed as a form of resistance to slavery in Brazil and practiced all around the world today. Capoeira, which is thriving in Bahia, is shown in *Segundo Sol* as part of exotic transition scenes, and as such provides opportunities to dissect and focus on the Black male body and form through close ups and slow motion. In this way, I argue, Capoeira in *Segundo Sol* not only helps perpetuate the hypersexual and virile Black body stereotype, but also serves as a marker class (lower class). Due to the entwined relationship between social class and race, it is no surprise that in *Segundo Sol,* capoeiristas (those who practice the art) are lower class, Black or mixed, even though today the art is practiced all over the world by all races and social class. The representation of Capoeira in *Segundo Sol* suggests an othering of the art, making it strange, deviant, and different in a hierarchical politicized way.

Finally, the conclusion offers a summary of the findings of this analysis. This includes both the changes and continuities in discourses of race in Brazil and its representation in telenovelas, as well as the role of telenovelas in such constructions, one that renders Brazilian society largely monochromatic. I also restate how representations in telenovelas go beyond "good" or "bad," but are a key aspect, or "building block" to the construction of identity since the genre ignites debate about "what it means to be . . . " Thus, while *Duas Caras* was a breakthrough telenovela for presenting audiences with its first Black protagonist on a major TV Globo telenovela, and *Segundo Sol* practically erased the existence of Blacks in Bahia, both programs contributed to a lively discussion of race and racism in contemporary Brazil.

NOTES

1. Although some affirmative action laws began to slowly be introduced in the country since the early 1990s, it was not until 2001 that the state of Rio de Janeiro made history when they adopted Brazil's first affirmative action policies governing university admissions, requiring the two state-run universities to reserve half of their admissions spots for graduates of public high schools (traditionally made up of lower-class and racial minorities), and 40 percent for Afro-Brazilians (traditionally underrepresented in Brazilian higher education). Additionally, in 2004 a system of quotas was also implemented for Brazilian television—requiring a minimum of 25 percent of afro descendant actors on TV programs and theatrical plays, and 40 percent in commercials on TV and movie theaters.

2. I should note that the 9 p.m. telenovela spot, is still the number one program as far as ratings in Brazil (Lopes & Greco, 2018).

3. The 12 countries gathered by Obitel network are Argentina, Brazil, Chile, Colombia, Ecuador, Spain, United States, Mexico, Peru, Portugal, Uruguay, and Venezuela.

4. See Martín Barbero, J. Challenges for communication research in Latin America Communication and Culture, 9, 1982, pp. 99–113; Martín Barbero, J.. From Media to Mediations: Communication, Culture and Hegemony, Mexico City, Ediciones G. Gili, 1987; Martín Barbero, J. Communication from Culture: The Crisis of the National and the Emergence of the Popular. Media, Culture and Society, 10, 1988, pp. 447–465; Martín-Barbero, J. Communication, Culture and Hegemony: From Media to Mediations, London; Newbury Park, Sage, 1993. Additionally, see García Canclini, N.. Consumers and Citizens: Globalization and Multicultural Conflicts. Minneapolis, The University of Minnesota Press, 2001.

Chapter One

From Active to Active-ism

Before exploring the relationship between—and transition from—audiences to active-ists, it is important to trace the historical, social, economic, and political roles played by Brazilian telenovelas not only in Brazil, but in a globalized televisual space. To do so, I begin this chapter by situating the telenovela text in the British Cultural Studies tradition (Hall, 1993) and the Latin American Media and Cultural Studies tradition (Martín-Barbero, 1993; García Canclini, 2001). I then trace changes in how audiences have viewed and participated in reading texts, including telenovela texts, as well as changes in the production and consumption of telenovelas. This exploration involves using Henry Jenkin's (2004; 2006) conception of convergence, pointing out that while Martín-Barbero's writings were mostly based on broadcasting media, they can certainly be reinterpreted to new media formats in order to enrich theories on interactive media, digital communication, and cultural convergence (Scolari, 2015, p. 1093). My analysis also examines concepts such as the "open text," a key characteristic of Brazilian telenovelas, and Brazilians' persistent affinity for the traditional television set as a mode of viewership. Finally, I discuss how advancements in technology have allowed the audience to not just be active viewers in Stuart Hall's sense of the term, but to also be "activists" (using the pun "active-ists") and cowriters of discourses about race and racism in contemporary Brazil. I finish the chapter with an example of this activism by spotlighting the campaign #EuPoderiaEstarEmSegundoSol (#ICouldbeinSegundoSol).

TELENOVELAS AS TEXT

The present analysis of the representation of Blacks in Brazilian primetime telenovelas borrows from Stuart Hall's (1993) Encoding/Decoding model, which grew out of the British Cultural Studies tradition. Thus, it is an interpretive comparative investigation of such representation: I am comparing and contrasting two major programs that aired in distinct contexts (ten years apart) and using textual analysis to define problematic and/or lingering portrayals and stereotypes. I am also using Hall's model to explore changes in and possibilities of such representations, as well as to suggest alternatives. The chapter additionally draws historical parallels between the portrayals of Brazilian and American Blacks in their respective visual media environments.

Hall's Encoding/Decoding model understands the interpretive approach by giving power to audiences to create their own meanings from texts. It identifies viewers as occupying one of three hypothetical positions as readers of a media text: First, audiences could engage in a *preferred reading*, where they decode media messages in the way that was intended by its producers. Second, they could engage in a *negotiated reading*, where they largely accept the preferred reading while simultaneously resisting and modifying it in order to account for their own subjective experiences. Finally, viewers could engage in an *oppositional reading* of media texts: here it is understood that the social position of the reader—their ethnicity, class, race, gender, sexuality, and so on—situates them in direct opposition to the mainstream interpretation of that same text. In other words, Hall reminds us that media texts are a site of hegemonic struggle, of negotiation and reconfiguration of popular culture and identity.

Latin American scholars also acknowledge the active role of audiences in interpreting media texts, as well as emphasize the need to look beyond the manipulative and commercial role of the media in order to understand the many ways meaning is created, experienced, consumed, and so forth (Garcia Canclíni, 2001; Martin-Barbero, 1993). The Latin American Media and Cultural Studies tradition investigates the very nature of communication, described by Martín-Barbero & Muñoz (1992) as a "web of words and desires, memories and structures of feelings, social divisions and cultural discontinuities, appropriations and media resistance and with which people weave their daily lives" (p. 6). Additionally, Martín-Barbero, reminds us to shift our focus away from technological determinism—the object itself—and toward the mediations, or the social processes that happen with encounters with media texts: the place from which it is possible to perceive and understand the interactions between the space of production and the space of reception (Scolari, 2015, p. 1098).

These theoretical frameworks highlight how telenovelas go far beyond being pure melodramas and are more than simply vehicles for ideological and consumer manipulation. Indeed, while critics have suggested that the telenovela genre is always entangled with the interests and desires of those whom corporations and or governments seek to entice (Dávila, 2001, pp. 14–15), Martín-Barbero (1993) states that telenovelas are a site of contestation and struggle over meanings and retain the traces of a popular culture that has resisted the direct imposition of dominant forms. At this point, a distinction needs to be made between the Anglo and Latin American understandings of "popular culture." While in the United States "popular" and "mass" culture can be considered as synonyms, in Latin America "mass culture" refers to homogenized "Culture Industry products," as described by Adorno & Horkheimer (2002). By contrast, "popular culture" relates to the folkloric culture, preindustrial culture, and/or the culture of subaltern classes, from Antonio Gramsci's perspective. Thus, Martín-Barbero suggests thinking about social identity in relation to popular culture without forgetting that popular culture has deeply modified the forms of expression of mass culture (Scolari, 2015, p. 1095).

In thinking about telenovelas in the context of popular vs. mass culture, it is important to note that, in Brazil and most of Latin America, telenovelas play a big role in the daily lives of those who watch them and even those who do not. This is because telenovelas are not just newsworthy, but actually function as agenda setters for news reports in various journalistic media (Joyce & Martinez, 2016). They are a key cultural product that can bring national audiences (in whichever country they are being shown daily) together (p. 87). In the following analysis, I therefore understand telenovelas as commercial products that make a lot of money selling not only ideological values, but also selling actual material products in a capitalist consumer society. I also rely on García-Canclini's (2001) insight that viewers look for clues and rules of democracy in such commercial products. Thus, as the author states because of this, consumption can be a place of cognitive value, and it can be good to think and act in a meaningful way that renews social life.

Telenovelas are, on the one hand, a powerful, global social force that impact individuals' social reality. On the other hand, however, they are also products that have been influenced by the contexts in which they were produced, reflecting the material, cultural, and social conditions of the communities in which texts originated. They create consumers and communities, function as venues for social messages and marketing, and reinforce and challenge the status quo (Rios & Castañeda, 2011, pp. 6–7). Finally, akin to Joyce & Martinez's (2019a) investigation of the representation of Blacks on the American television program *Parenthood*, an essential component of the present analysis is the understanding of consumption as a form of engagement and practice of politics in the context of free market corporate media, despite the lack of contemporary trust in political representatives (p. 271). This is an important aspect of active audiences, active-ists, mediations, and, in the current digital technology environment, what Scolari (2015) refers to as "hypermediations," a concept that will be addressed below.

Telenovelas as Brazilian Text

The first Brazilian telenovela aired in 1951, just one year after the medium arrived in that country. Seventy years later, they are still thriving locally and globally. As Rios and Castañeda (2011) suggest, these televisual cultural products are gaining ever greater importance because they embody the ultimate crossover phenomenon: they penetrate global markets with a proven commercial product while simultaneously giving pleasure to audiences (p. 4). TV Globo, with its particular patriarchal dynastic character has dominated not just the Brazilian market but the international market as well. As Joyce & La Pastina (2020) write, in Brazil, giant media dynasties rely on virtual and horizontal integration, which

> has led to the development of a monopoly in the broadcasting industry. The two new major players in "pay TV" are TVA (owned by the publishing group, Abril) and Globosat (TV Globo). Additionally, Globo's broadcast signal can be picked up in 99.5% of the Brazilian territory, and for over thirty years, its own international channel, Globo Internacional, has distributed programs to more than 130 countries (over 300 telenovelas). Additionally, in 2007, twenty-five thousand hours of programming were licensed in over fifty countries and translated into twenty-four different languages, reaching an average audience of 100 million viewers worldwide every day (p. 39).

Telenovelas are a staple of TV programming in Brazil. One cannot refer to the former without bringing up the latter. Broadcast daily (Monday–Saturday) on a never-ending carousel style of production and consumption, the ending of one telenovela in a given timeslot is immediately followed by the start of a new one in that same slot, with no hiatus in between. Although the following fact is out of the historical scope of the present research as far as the years which are being examined—from 2008 to 201—it is noteworthy to point out that while due to the COVID-19 pandemic, 2021 was the first time in history that a Brazilian telenovela paused production, and reruns were aired instead of original episodes.

Another characteristic of Brazilian telenovelas are their length and number of episodes. While telenovela series traditionally lasted for at least one year, due to global trends in viewership, another recent development that should be noted is that in 2019 TV Globo's director of dramaturgy Silvio de Abreu announced that programs on that station would be shortened by an average of forty episodes in all timeslots (Ricco, 2019, para 4–6). However, despite this new institutionalized format, the fact remains that what really determines the length of a telenovela in Brazil is the show's ratings, or what is commonly known as "Ibope points," the Brazilian equivalent of Nielsen ratings. Ibope (*Instituto Brasileiro de Opinião Pública e Estatística* /Brazilian Institute of

Public Opinion and Statistics) was established in 1942 and has since become the official ratings system in the country. Since the 1980s, Ibope points have been powerful enough to determine the life or death of telenovela characters and of programs themselves (Joyce, 2013, p. 59).

Another aspect of Brazilian telenovelas that distinguishes them from the genre in other countries is what is described as "the open text," an important production characteristic that allows last minute changes to the plot when there is commotion, public discontent, and or controversies. This is perhaps best exemplified by the public outcry over the perceived racism due to the lack of Black representation in the promo for *Segundo Sol*. The ongoing daily production of "chapters," as episodes are called in Brazil, allow producers and writers to keep the narrative open to (literally) last minute changes. As an open text, a program is in direct and constant conversation with the audiences that watch it, industry and audience marketing strategies, outcomes, and so forth, changing and adapting to current events and situations.

While in the past TV Globo used focus groups and industry chatter to gauge reactions and implement changes in their texts on an ongoing basis, nowadays technological advancements such as the popularity and heavy use of social media allow audiences to influence the "open texts" of telenovelas more than ever before. This tremendous influence of social media is what we witnessed during the controversy surrounding the *Segundo Sol* and the reaction and consequent activism against the lack of Black bodies on the promo for the upcoming narrative. I should also note that although Brazilian audiences have not abandoned their beloved TV set as their go-to device for watching telenovelas, they do transition from screen to screen in a comple-mentary way as we will see with our case study and as discussed by Jenkins (2006). Indeed, growing internet use has not led to the abandonment of the traditional television set in Brazil, but to a process of transmediations and a distinct relationship between "old-new" media screens. Additionally, beyond the transition between old and new technology, we should also note that the most popular genre in Brazil is "old." Therefore, even with all the advance-ments in technology and easy access to streaming programs from all over the world, which have undoubtedly fragmented the traditional TV viewing public, in Brazil, TV Globo's telenovelas are still the number one locally produced program of production and consumption and can reach 100 million people a day—which is about half of the country's population (Kaiser, 2019, para 20).[1]

As noted above, a key ingredient to the longevity of Brazilian telenovelas is the "open text," which amongst other things creates an alliance between the show and a diverse audience, giving viewers a sense that they are cowriters of the programs they watch. One consequence of this relationship, however, is that when the alliance breaks down, such as in the case of the perceived racism in *Segundo Sol*, viewers can go to the Internet and use social media to voice their concerns. Thus, it is important for this analysis to look at transmediation not only in the traditional way as proposed by Jenkins (2006), but also as the movement of audience members from viewers and readers (i.e., from consumers of meaning) to active-ists, online creating and challenging hegemonic meanings conveyed by telenovelas, creating their own texts, voices, and spaces, and pressuring corporations and lawmakers to listen to their cry for inclusivity, diversity, and to end racism.

As Joyce and La Pastina (2020) show, perhaps the most striking example of the "open text" and its malleability took place in 2006, during the final episodes of the primetime telenovela *Velho Chico* ("Old Chico"). *Velho Chico* a rural telenovela set by the São Francisco River (aka "Old Chico") and travelled back and forth through three different time periods. However, due to the tragic death of the leading male actor Domingos Montagner, who played the character of Santo, during the filming of the last few episodes of the telenovela, a postmortem subjective camera—was the quick fix used to keep the character alive in the narrative. All of this was made possible by the "open text." *Velho Chico* signaled the first time the open text was not only used as a textual device, but as an innovative production aesthetic strategy.

As noted by the Joyce and La Pastina (2020), *Velho Chico*'s production strategy positioned viewers in the place (POV) of the leading actor, disrupting their traditional place as viewers/readers of the telenovela text:

> When characters in the program talked to Santo, they were in fact talking to the audience via direct address. The subjective camera disrupted traditional ways of making telenovelas and represented a new and interesting type of audience inclusion that represents aesthetically, what has been suggested in general about Brazilian telenovelas: that as an open text, the program is in direct and constant conversation with the audiences that watch them, and that these strategies change and adapt to current events (p. 39).

While in the past, when tragic real-life events prevented actors from filming, writers would simply find a way to write them out of the story by either killing them, sending them on a trip, or otherwise removing them from the central narrative. But never before had audience members taken the actual place of a character: they saw things through Santo's "eyes" and heard dialogue "for" Santo. This was made possible because when various characters—his love interest, daughter, brothers—talked to Santo, they looked straight into the camera (Santo and/or viewers) in a direct address. The character was able to engage with others and participate in the narrative through camera movements, through filming techniques that used blurred focus to represent tears in emotional situations and muddled vision and through the use of prerecorded audio by Montagner (Joyce and La Pastina, 2020, pp. 39–43). The strategy of "standing in for the actor" resonated with audiences who immediately, by the thousands, expressed their approval of this production decision online, causing Domingos Montagner's name along with comments citing the "subjective camera" to become a trending topic on twitter during the broadcast (Dos Santos, 2016, para 2). This exchange between the two screens reminds us of what Jenkins (2004) describes as "convergence culture," one amongst various components of the activism stemming from *Segundo Sol*'s promo, which will be further developed below.

FROM MEDIA AND MEDIATIONS TO TRANSMEDIA AND HYPERMEDIATIONS; AND FROM ACTIVE TO ACTIVE-ISTS

As we have seen, mediation theory explored the tensions and mutual appropriations of mass and popular culture, built around a specific historical period in the 1980s and revolving around analog technologies. But as Scolari (2015) states, with digital technologies the manipulation, reproduction, and exchange of information on a global scale is facilitated and exacerbated. Thus, Scolari contends that in this context hypermediations focus on the tensions and mutual appropriations of participatory and digital mass culture, or what Jenkins (2004) described as convergence culture. In this new context, hypermediations ask us to forget the new object (new media) and to investigate the social transformations that new forms of communication generate. In this sense, this new perspective does not negate the previous one, but rather builds on it by focusing on the new social processes and experiences (Scolari, 2017, pp. 1099–1101).

In this new context of hypermediations, it is important to focus on the new experiences. I also suggest it is imperative to examine the texts that precede such encounters and processes. Therefore, we should focus on two additional concepts that make up current telenovelas' texts: convergence and transmedia storytelling. As Jenkins (2006) explains, convergence is understood as a series of intersections between different media systems that go beyond the technological meeting of different media and media content by also including the relationship between the media industry and popular culture, which brings an unprecedented number of participatory opportunities for audiences to become producers of messages.

From the media industry's perspective, Jenkins (2006) identifies a key component in this new environment: transmedia storytelling, or the process through which essential elements of a narrative get distributed systematically across multiple delivery channels for the purpose of creating a unified and coordinated entertainment experience, with each medium making its individual contribution to the unfolding of a narrative. Convergence, then, is optimized by the synergy that is provided by horizontal and vertical integrations present in media giants such as TV Globo. Consequently, convergence repositions the passive viewer of television—in the sense that they passively receive messages from a medium (not in Hall's sense of how they decode such messages)—to what Jenkins describes as that of an active "hunter/gatherer," a viewer/consumer/producer of content. In other words, the audience moves from the invisible margins of popular culture into the center of current thinking about media production and consumption (p. 12).

When *Segundo Sol* aired in 2018, TV Globo had already been experimenting with convergence for several years, since their telenovelas had been available for streaming to Brazilian and international fans since 2000. As Rêgo (2011) states, TV Globo pioneered the strategy of making daily segments of its programs available online and free of charge on its website. It also provided viewers with the option of having access to full-length programming through a monthly subscription, an approach that helped, rather than hindered broadcast viewership at home, while simultaneously increasing the network's global marketing and promotion capacities (p. 87).

In addition to convergence and the increasingly complex way in which information circulates between viewers (active-ists) and producers, there is also another contextual example that I should address as it relates to online activism toward racial equality and to the zeitgeist in which the telenovela Segundo Sol and the social activism about it took place. The year 2018, when *Segundo Sol* aired with inadequate Black representation, was also the fifth anniversary of the hashtag #BlackLivesMatter. According to a Pew Research Center (2018) analysis of public tweets using Crimson Hexagon software, the #BlackLivesMatter hashtag first appeared on Twitter in July 2013 following the acquittal of George Zimmerman in the shooting death of Trayvon Martin in Florida. From July 2013 through May 1, 2018, the hashtag was used nearly 30 million times on Twitter, an average of 17,002 times per day (Anderson, Toor, Rainie & Smith, 2018, para 1). The hashtag #BlackLivesMatter is an archetypal example of a hashtag tied to a political issue or cause that has maintained a high baseline level of usage on Twitter over a period of several years.[2] Many other hashtags related to various causes, events, or political issues evolve in a variety of ways, some only lasting a few days or months, while others can have a type of rebirth on anniversaries associated with the hashtag, for example #MeToo, #JeSuisCharlie, and #LoveWins (Anderson et al, 2018, para 6).

The Brazilian #EuPoderiaEstarEmSegundoSol is an interesting example of a hashtag used to highlight social issues that originated as a direct response to a telenovela text: a text that seemingly erased Blacks from the television screen and from Bahia society. As soon as the promo for the upcoming tele-novela was released, viewers went to the program's official site to point out the racism of only having white actors on the telenovela with comments such as "is this telenovela shot in Europe?" (Junior, 2018, para 3). In this case, the text of a mere promo spurred viewers to question it and immediately turned them from active viewers to online activists. As one news story summarized:

> Globo's next telenovela, "Segundo Sol," has not yet premiered, but it is already causing controversy on social networks because of the absence of Blacks in its cast. Set in Bahia, the plot was criticized for only choosing white actors (Segundo Sol: ausência, 2018, para 1).

The news report also highlighted the beginning of the campaign #EuPoderiaEstarEmSegundoSol, that was initially created and promoted by the Facebook page "Trick Tudo" to point out racism and to highlight the fact that there could have been representation of Black bodies and culture on the program by sharing a list of fifty Black actors known to have been cast in TV Globo telenovelas in the past. Within three days, the Facebook post listing the possible Black cast members received more than twenty-five thousand likes (Segundo Sol: ausência, 2018, para 2).

Across various online platforms, multiple social actors/activists criticized the telenovela promo text for being racist due to the sheer lack of Black bod-ies it featured. But many also pointed out North-South regionalism charac-teristic of Brazilian society also present in telenovelas: generally speaking, southern states are usually more industrialized and white and perceived as "better" than the more rural and racially mixed states in the northern coun-terparts. Additionally, activists criticized the lack of actual Bahian actors in *Segundo Sol*, with their characteristic accent; this was particularly problem-atic as the white actors playing Bahians had southeast accents and adopted terrible "fake" accents from Bahia. This was highlighted in a post on TV Globo's website where one activist pointed out that: "Their accent changes according to their wardrobe change. At times it is from Bahia, at others from Rio." This commentator also asked the rhetorical question: "Is Bahia in Europe? Salvador is one of the cities with the most Blacks in the world, and yet there are not enough Blacks to represent our land" (Segundo Sol é criticada, 2018, para 4).

With active-ism in full force, TV Globo felt the need to address the matter. A few days after the initial Facebook post, the network issued a public state-ment emphasizing that the broadcaster does not cast their programs based on actors' "skin color." Specifically, TV Globo stated that: "The selection criteria for a telenovela are technical and artistic. Globo does not guide the casting of its works by skin color, but by the suitability to the character's profile, talent and availability of the cast. And we believe that this is the most correct way to do that" (Após críticas, 2018, para 1). The statement, which seemed to imply that Black actors were not talented enough, led a group of Black actors to immediately seek a meeting with network executives and to question this assertion. In a meeting a few days later with Monica Albuquerque, TV Globo's Director of Development and Artistic Monitoring (Diretora de Desenvolvimento e Acompanhamento Artístico), Albuquerque acknowledged there was a problem and vowed to work on it. By recognizing that there was in fact "less representativeness than we would like," Globo came to adopt a more flexible position than it had demonstrated earlier that week when the controversy first erupted (Styler, 2018, para 1–3).

Importantly, the second public statement published by TV Globo acknowledged that the network was making changes and addressing the issue due to net-activism by stating, amongst other things, that the meeting with Monica Albuquerque took place in order to discuss the "company's positioning in regards to the critical comments about the telenovela line-up that circulated on social networks over the weekend" (para 8).

The interplay between various social actors—industry representatives, active-ists, government bodies, and lawmakers—coupled with the flexibility of the telenovela's open text, led to a lively discussion about race and racism in Brazil. It also produced immediate, actual change. For example, Actress Roberta Rodrigues, who is Afro-Brazilian, was cast for the role that had initially been intended for Carol Castro, who is white. This recasting marks the "first record of substitution of a white actress for a Black one in the history of Brazilian dramaturgy" (Castro e Guaraldo, 2017, para 1).

At the height of the controversy ignited by the net activism, Denis Carvalho, Artistic Director of *Segundo Sol*, was questioned about the lack of representation of Blacks in TV Globo productions in general, and especially in this particular telenovela. He responded that he did not want to revisit the issue, since TV Globo had already addressed it publicly. But he nonetheless defended his casting decisions by stating that the type of internet pressure the network was experiencing had no previous precedent, but now presented itself due to the power of social networks, where debates and polemics quickly gain strength. He added that above all TV Globo was making fiction, not a documentary, which should allow for some creative licenses (Chefão da Globo, 2018, para 3).

Another immediate consequence of the online activism was that it prompted the Public Ministry of Labour (Ministério Público do Trabalho (MPT) to fine TV Globo and to send them official recommendations detailing changes that needed to be made regarding representation of Black actors in *Segundo Sol* (Travae, 2018b, para 8–10). Moreover, this controversy inspired the MPT to go a step further and to also send similar notifications to two other major networks—Record and SBT—criticizing the lack of representation of the Black population in their productions. The document proposed a series of solutions to contribute to increasing diversity at the broadcasters, including having a census of workers who provide services to networks and promoting programming that raises awareness about racism in Brazil (Depois da Globo, 2018, para 1).

Highlighting the seriousness with which the MPT took the issue, Valdirene Silva de Assis, the MPT's National Coordinator for the Promotion of Equality, stated that other notifications like the one sent to the above-mentioned networks would be sent to all other networks, because the dialogue about race that the Public Ministry of Labour intended to establish should spread to all other channels, "who have their licenses through public concession, and have the social responsibility and an important role in the formation, construction, consolidation and alteration of stereotypes about the role of Blacks in Brazilian society, something that is very relevant in the discussion regarding structural racism" (Depois da Globo, 2018, para 3).

Despite the steps taken by the MPT, and changes in casting following the controversy surrounding the trailer of *Segundo Sol*, criticism and net-activism focused on the telenovela text and the "white Bahia" portrayed in the show persisted throughout the broadcast of *the telenovela*: they did not die down once the program started airing. TV Globo constantly added Black bodies to the subplots of the narrative throughout the program's run in a way that seemed forced according to some critics, as every "extra" that was inserted in the telenovela was Black, a nontraditional strategy utilized by the network. This had the effect of simply calling more attention to the lack of Black principal characters, prompting a news report by the national newspaper *A Folha de São Paulo to* point out that while every minor "extra" character on *Segundo Sol* was Black—including an assistant at an engineering firm, a bank manager, a real estate agent, and a lawyer—all the main actors continued to not only be white, but in fact to be blond (Após Críticas à Bahia Branca, 2018, para 1–9).

A final noteworthy change brought about by the active-ists and the national debate about race and racism that they ignited was the fact that amidst the controversy, TV Globo announced that they would produce an end of the year TV special using only local Bahian actors, directors, and writers. The production was set to be made in a partnership between Globo Filmes (Globo's cinematographic arm) and TV Bahia, an affiliate of the broadcaster in the state of Bahia (Após críticas por telenovela branca, 2019, para 1).

As the *Segundo Sol* controversy and the subsequent steps taken by both government and TV Globo illustrate, active-ists were able to produce a lively public discussion and debate about race and racism in Brazil, achieved with the assistance of several social actors. They were also able to rewrite the status quo text about what it means to be Black and to a certain extent to even exist as Black in Brazil and not be erased. They effectively made the case that Black bodies, culture, and stories belonged in the narrative of tele-novelas, especially those set in predominately Black regions. But what type of representations were created? Was there a reliance on stereotypes? What types of texts were offered about what it means to be Black in Brazil and in Bahia? These are some of the questions that will be addressed in the upcoming chapters.

CONCLUSION

This chapter has examined Brazilian telenovelas from the perspectives of the British Cultural Studies (Hall, 1993) and Latin American Media and Cultural Studies traditions (Martín-Barbero, 1993; García Canclini, 2001), and situated them in the contemporary context of what Jenkins (2004; 2006) refers to as convergence culture. It also discussed the history of Brazilian telenovelas as a cultural product and a genre, as well as its evolution, from its origins as a product for domestic consumption to becoming a powerful player in a globalized television and streaming market, or what Rêgo (2011) refers to as "from humble beginnings to International Prominence" (p. 75). Finally, the chapter explored the transition between active audiences to active-ists by examining the influential campaign #EuPoderiaEstarEmSegundoSol.

Stuart Hall's model was used to examine the text and its readers as active; when it comes to the telenovela, Hall's encoding/decoding model gives audiences the power to create their own meanings out of the texts they receive by placing them in three hypothetical positions as readers of mediated communication: preferred, negotiated, and oppositional. This model reminds us that media texts are sites of hegemonic struggle, of negotiation, and of the reconfiguration of popular culture and identity.

Martín-Barbero's (1993) theory focused on Latin America's broadcasting media and likewise highlighted the active role of audiences, urging us to shift our focus away from technological determinism—the object itself—and toward the moments and social processes that happen through encounters with media texts. In other words, the approach goes "from media, to mediations," or the place between the space of production and the space of reception (Scolari, 2015, p. 1098).

Jenkin's (2004, 2006) concept of convergence culture brings about the processes of transmediations and transmedia storytelling, highlighting a distinct relationship between old and new media screens, and eventually leading to what I described as the evolution from active and active-its: the movement of audience members from viewers and readers of meaning to creators and challengers of hegemonic meanings and texts. This progression involves the opening up of spaces for viewers' own voices and representations, and pressuring corporations and law makers to listen and to act, in this case with regards to matters of inclusivity, diversity, and racism.

Thus, as we have seen, in our current technological digital environment there is an ongoing shift from mediations to hypermediations, and a shifting focus on the tensions and mutual appropriations of participatory and digital mass culture. Or, as Scolari (2015) states, in the current environment we shift focus away from the (new) object (new media) and toward the social transformations that these new forms of communication generate (pp. 1099–1101).

One such transformation examined here was the campaign #EuPoderiaEstarEmSegundoSol—a reaction against the racism in the upcoming telenovela: one that was set in the state with the highest concentration of Blacks in Brazil, but with an absence of Black actors. Here we witnessed a move from active to active-ists, and discussed a few examples of immediate changes to the telenovela text and to the overall discourse about race in Brazil ignited by such activism. Changes highlighted included the inclusion of more Black actors and story lines in upcoming programs in response to pressure by the Public Ministry of Labor, and creating additional programming set in Bahia made by an all Bahian cast and crew.

As I have argued in this chapter, the link between the telenovela and its audience is best described as "interactive, since the impact of telenovelas on viewers is matched by the impact of viewers on them" (Page, 1995, p. 448). This reciprocity means that telenovelas serve as sites of debate which bridge the gap between private and public spheres. As I argued in my previous book *Brazilian Telenovelas and the Myth of Racial Democracy* (Joyce, 2012), telenovelas texts are a vital, vibrant space for examining racism and the representation of Black Brazilians specifically, and society more generally. The controversy surrounding the airing of *Segundo Sol* in 2018, and the consequences of that controversy, show that this remains true a decade later. Telenovela texts continue to: ignite debate, generate questions about matters of race and identity, and produce social change.

NOTES

1. In 2015 among the top ten most viewed programs in Brazil, seven were telenovelas (Lopes & Gómes, 2015, pp. 28, 25, 59).

2. According to Pew, the use of #BlackLivesMatter peaked in 2020, three days after George Floyd died in police custody: #BlackLivesMatter was tweeted 8.8 million times that day; for the following two weeks, users tweeted #BlackLivesMatter

an average of nearly 3.7 million times per day. Before that, the use of the hashtag had peaked in summer 2016, when it was mentioned around 500,000 times daily (Anderson, 2020, para 2 and 6).

Chapter Two

Her Body

From Baby Mamma to Mammie

This chapter offers an analysis of the portrayal of Afro-Brazilian women across the two productions—*Duas Caras* and *Segundo Sol*. It will focus primarily on the representation of the *Segundo Sol* character Zefa, the aging light-skinned Afro-Brazilian maid who worked her entire life for a successful and traditional white family in Bahia—the Athayde family. The textual/character analysis I offer is part of a scholarly conversation about the representation of Blacks in Brazil, but also explores differences in how Blacks are represented in the American and Brazilian visual media. In this sense, the present chapter builds on my previous investigation of the representation of Blacks in *Brazilian Telenovelas and the Myth of Racial Democracy* (2012), as well as Araújo's (2004) study *A Negação do Brasil*, where the author analyzed the representation of Brazilian Blacks in telenovelas between 1960 and 1990. Those studies conversed with Bogle's (2001) *Toms, coons, mulattoes, mammies, and bucks: An interpretive history of Blacks in American films*, as does the current analysis.

The present investigation reveals that although some progress has been made in terms of how Blacks are portrayed in Brazilian telenovelas in recent decades, there unfortunately remains a heavy reliance on the stereotypes identified by the previous research. It is noteworthy that in 2005 TV Globo gained a mention in the *Guinness World of Records* for being the world's largest producer of telenovelas with 300 titles at the time. This position has remained the same, thus the question of how they represent Afro-Brazilians and Afro-Brazilian culture is important, as it helps us to understand popular notions of "what it means to be . . . " This chapters offers an analysis of the portrayal of Afro-Brazilian women, across the two productions—*Duas Caras* and *Segundo Sol*, but more specifically, this chapter offers a close reading of the character Zefa.

As we have seen, *Segundo Sol* is a story that spans two decades with jumps between the future and the past. At times, it uses different actors to portray "younger versions of themselves." At other times, viewers are left to imagine what these characters looked like in the past based on the narratives and "back stories" about them that the show provides. Zefa is one of the characters who was narratively present in all the timelines covered by the program. She is an extremely interesting character for analysis because, in her role as an older Black woman in a telenovela narrative that "jumped 20 years into the future" to represent the present time (2018), she embodies what Bogle (2001) identified as "Mammie" figure, or what Araújo (2004) termed "Mamãe": the mother of all, extremely nurturing and subservient. Indeed, Zefa in the contemporary story line (2018) provides a textbook representation of almost all the main traits of the Mammie figure: at this stage in her life, she is a mature woman, heavier set, matronly, desexualized, loving, and nonthreatening.

However, whereas the contemporary plot portrayed Zefa as a Mammie, the same is not true for the plotline twenty years prior. In that period, as a younger woman, Zefa was her white boss's server not only in the kitchen but in master bedroom as well. Here, we can classify Zefa as embodying another traditional stereotype applied to Black women: the mixed-Black female or Mulatta (Mitchell, 2020), or the hypersexual Jezebel (Boylorn, 2008). Both these stereotypes apply simultaneously due to the fact that, phenotypically, Zefa is a light-skinned Black woman, but one who also has a sexually available body and a voracious appetite for sex, which are familiar tropes used to portray young Black women in both Brazilian and American media. This brings our South/North comparison of media representations of Blackness closer still since, as Boylorn (2008) indicates, in the United States "Black women on television fall into historical categories of stereotypes that range from the hypersexual Jezebel to the asexual Mammie, and contemporary versions of each." Zefa embodies all of these categories of stereotypes, as I will demonstrate below.

It is noteworthy that both in Brazil and the United States, two countries that share a history and legacy of slavery, Black women have been encoded in similar ways in visual media. As Boylorn (2008, pp. 413–433) states, Black women on American TV are generally represented through stereotypes. He suggests that they should use an oppositional reading when decoding television texts that are (supposedly) about themselves (this is akin to Stuart Hall's [1993] discussion of television texts in the previous chapter). Thus, while racist imagery of Blacks in Brazilian and American media is readily available, and seems to be the norm in many genres, decoding messages about race in an empowering way is an act of resistance that requires work ("oppositional reading"). And while Boylorn (2008) suggests that on American TV Black women are usually represented according to binaries of either/or—such as extremely educated or high school dropouts; ambitious or lazy; sexy or ugly (pp. 413–433)—I use Zefa as an example of a Black body that embodies two major yet seemingly contradictory stereotypes: The Mammie and the Jezebel/Mulatta. That the same character can embody both these stereotypes highlights another oppressive intersection at work in her portrayal: ageism.

Also relevant to the analysis in this chapter is Boylorn's (2008) observation that, in America, Black women's televized relationships with a man are always scary because she is either too polite and independent to need or want a man, or because she is desperate and lost without him. Consequently, these extreme and false representations of what it means to be a Black woman on television leave limited opportunities for them to be represented outside such prescribed boundaries (pp. 413–433). This is a lingering problematic representation and imagined racial construction that has been persistent in Brazil as well, and which we can see in the character Zefa.

As previously discussed, when it comes to Bogle's (2001) classifications of American Blacks in visual culture, also demonstrated by Joyce (2012) in *Duas Caras*, a common way of representing older Black female bodies is through the Mammie trope. This is also true in *Segundo Sol* with "Mammie Zefa": her role in the narrative is clear: she is the older, kind, heavier set Black woman, who takes care of her employer's white family as her own and may be considered a part of the household, albeit a non-white one, who is also relegated to the maid's quarters when her bosses do not need her services and wish to make her invisible.

But Zefa is a peculiar character for various reasons. For example, while the protagonists of *Segundo Sol* are white, we can clearly identify who the Black leading actors/roles are, as they have speaking lines, complex story lines, recurring appearances, but most importantly, due to the fact that their actions are directly influenced or influence those of the other (mostly white) leading characters. In this sense, in addition to being a Mammie, Zefa can also be considered the Afro-Brazilian female lead, as she is the mother of the Black male lead (under the same guidelines) and the figurative mother of the whole Athayde family.

HISTORICAL PORTRAYALS OF HER BLACK BODY

The first Mammie portrayal in Brazil can be traced back to the character *Mamãe Dolores*/Mother Dolores, who featured in the 1964 telenovela *O Direito de Nascer*/ "The Right to be Born" (Joyce, 2006, p. 48), and obviously embodied the Mammie stereotype. Thus, a lingering stereotype, since for one of the most striking aspects of Zefa's character is that she was a Black housekeeper that gave her white-skinned son to her white employers to raise as their own but kept her Black-skinned son to herself. But the original Mammie, Mamãe Dolores was by no means the protagonist in her telenovela. This would not happen until decades later in 2004, when actress Taís Araújo became the first Black actress to be the protagonist in a telenovela, starring in *Da Cor do Pecado/* "The Color of Sin," a title with obvious racial undertones. Later in 2009, Araújo was became the first Black female to be cast as the lead in a primetime telenovela, *Viver a Vida/* "Seize the Day" (September 14, 2009, to May 14, 2010) by writer Manoel Carlos. This casting was extremely significant not only because it marked the first time that viewers in Brazil were presented with an Afro-Brazilian woman in the leading role in a primetime program, but also because she was the first Black "Helena." Manoel Carlos is a traditional primetime telenovela hit-maker who usually tells a story of a hardworking heroine who overcomes many difficulties in her life, but who at the end of the program achieves personal and professional success. Although played by different actresses throughout the years, his protagonists are always called "Helena," with Taís Araújo being the sixth Helena in one of his productions. In addition to being the first Black Helena, the actress was also the youngest to play that role.

Prior to Araújo, all of Carlos' "Helenas" had been white, middle to upper class, successful women in their mid-forties and fifties. They were each sexually active and in search of love. The first Black Helena was a young runway model (Araújo was thirty in real life when she played the part), and her most distinctive characteristic was her physical beauty and attractive body type. I should also point out, however, that even though Araújo is Black, she is a light-skinned Black woman, known for her "small button nose," perhaps a reflection of her mixed Afro-European heritage (she is of Austrian, Portuguese, and African descent).

In *Viver a Vida*, Helena's romantic interest was Marcos, played by José Mayer, who is usually cast as the romantic lead in Brazilian telenovelas. In the plot and in real life, the age difference between them was twenty years. Marcos, a successful businessman, cannot resist Helena's beauty. She too falls for his charm, abandoning her successful career to become, in essence, his trophy wife. And while Helena may no longer work as a model, her striking physical beauty still drives the focus of the narrative. She can be accurately described as embodying popular media's representation of the Mulatta: a desired, beautiful, hypersexual object (Mitchell, 2020, p. 31).

It is important to note that as problematic as Helena's portrayal may have been, the decision to cast Araújo in the role was still a crucial moment for the representation and inclusion of Blacks in Brazilian media and social life. *Viver a Vida* aired in 2009 and 2010, a time when Brazil was undergoing political, economic, and social transformations toward racial inclusion, such as the beginning of a more systematic application of affirmative action policies throughout the country, especially in regards to racial quotas for students entering public universities. Perhaps not coincidently, also in 2009___ viewers also saw another woman of Afro-descendant as the lead role in a telenovela, although not a primetime program. Specifically, *Cama de Gato* ("Cat's Cradle"), broadcast in the six o'clock (pm) timeslot, featured actress Camila Pitanga playing a maid. Although she was employed in the program in a service role, she was the lead protagonist.

In 2015, Camila Pitanga was cast again as the protagonist in a telenovela, this one that aired in primetime, *Babylônia*/ "Babylon." This evidence of growing inclusion of Blacks in Brazilian TV also reflects the growth of the Afro-Brazilian middle class and of their increased buying power. According to Pereira Jr. (2012), between 2003 and 2011, about forty million non-white Brazilians entered the country's middle class, an economic and social phenomenon that is also linked to this population's access to affirmative action policies at universities, as well as in the job market. Even aside from concerns about social and racial justice, we can see that for TV Globo, it made commercial sense to have a larger number of Black people represented in its leading vehicle for advertising revenue—the telenovela.

MULATTA ZEFA

As mentioned above, Zefa offers us a unique example of a Black body which embodies traditional stereotypical tropes used in the representation of Black female bodies in visual media in both the United States and Brazil: Jezebels, Mulattas, and Mammies. This is due to a peculiar characteristic of *Segundo Sol*: the fact that the story line spans over a period of twenty years.

The following dialogue depicts this troubling representation and is a good illustration of the sacrificial love traditional given by Mammies, as well as of the appreciation that white characters and families bestow on such characters. It also reflects the stereotypical representation of the hypersexualized Black woman or "Jezebel" (Boylorn, 2008), or Mitchell's (2020) "Mulatta" trope. The following scene took place during the first week of the broadcast, in the episode that aired on May 17, 2018. The scene opens with Claudine Athayde, the white matriarch, having a "heart to heart" with Zefa, the family's housekeeper. The scene is set in the telenovela's "current time," or 2018. Claudine is extremely ill, and on the verge of death. She tells Zefa that they must talk, due to the fact that she "owes her life's happiness" to her "good friend Zefa" (*Segundo Sol*, May 17, 2018).

In a chiaroscuro scene with soft instrumental music, the two "friends" talk in the Master Bedroom, as Claudine invites Zefa to sit on the master bed beside her. Zefa is wondering how Claudine is feeling, to which Claudine replies that she is having a good day, but that the reality is, death is near. It is interesting to note that Claudine refers to Zefa as "my friend," while Zefa refers to her employer as "Madam," highlighting the power imbalance of the relationship. As the scene progresses, Claudine reminds Zefa (and reveals to the audience) that she "could not have kids," and that Zefa "gave me yours [hers] to be raised by me, as my own. I will never forget that Edgar[1] is your son. Born from you." Zefa humbly replies: "Please forget about this, madam, you take such good care of him, you love him so much. You raised him well." At this moment the soft instrumental music becomes more prominent and the scene is now shot in extreme close up of their faces, as they sit together, holding hands. Zefa has tears running down her face, while Claudine is calm and subdued. Claudine tells Zefa that she "taught her" how to love Edgar and that he is "their" son. She adds that Edgar loves Zefa like a mother, even without knowing that she is his "real mother" and that her "blood runs in his veins" (*Segundo Sol*, 05/17/2018).

As the dialogue continues, Zefa shakes her head, crying, and replies that "that is true." Claudine then reveals that she also loves Zefa's other son Roberval "very much," and that she feels a "mother's love for him." We must note that while the character makes this statement, the audience knows that Zefa's other son with her boss (and Claudine's husband), the Black-skinned Roberval, was raised in the kitchen, as the maid's son, and is currently the family's driver. In other words, he was always and continues to be viewed as having a servant status. By contrast, the white brother Edgar was raised as a member of the Athayde family, in the master's quarters. Claudine then reveals that she has "been thinking about all of this" and t believes "Roberval has the right to know that Edgar is his brother," and that "Severo, my husband, is his dad, and that he is an heir to all of this" (*Segundo Sol*, 05/17/2018).

At this moment, Zefa respectfully interrupts in a quiet voice, saying that they "should not dig up the past." To this, Claudine interjects saying that "this is what is just, Zefa." Again, Zefa tries to plead with her employer, arguing that Roberval "is happy with what he has" and that Claudine "has been generous with him." After all, the Athaydes paid for his schooling. Zefa then states, hopefully, that "My son will soon get a good job and become someone. You will see." Claudine replies that Zefa is a "better woman than she is" (*Segundo Sol*, 05/17/2018).

As we can observe in this emotionally charged scene, Zefa's world is the Athayde family's world. She does not have a life or identity outside of the white family and her role in the white household. She is literally stuck in the kitchen, a modern-day variation of the *senzala*, or slave quarters. Furthermore, it is assumed that Zefa was not only sexually harassed in the household, but in fact was exploited sexually and reproductively as she bore a son by her employer, and then "gave" her white-passing son[2] to her employers to raise as their own. Zefa's embodiment of the hypersexual, sexually available ste-reotype of the Mulatta is never more evident than in the same scene when Claudine actually thanks her for having had sex with her husband "all those years" ago, claiming that without Zefa's "help" she "would not have been able to handle her husband's sexual appetite" (*Segundo Sol*, May 17, 2018).

Among other things, this scene of dialogue between Claudine and Zefa exemplifies the intersectional nature of race-based and gender-based oppres-sion in Brazil, both historically and in the media. Specifically, Afro-Brazilian women have been relegated to a social structure that requires them to serve white elites both sexually and economically (Caldwell, 2007, pp. 19–20). The scene above is exemplary in this sense but is also one that is extremely com-plex to read/decode. It is a scene that takes an engaged viewer to enter Hall's encoding/decoding model. The relationship between Zefa and Claudine is portrayed as one of partnership, friendship, love, softness, and gratitude. This is conveyed through the calm and quiet tone in which they speak to one another, and the way in which they hold each other's hands and caress each other's faces, for example. Other production elements such as the soft instrumental background music, slow camera movements, and editing cuts, in addition to the extreme close-ups, also encode such meanings into the scene.

However, because Zefa was Claudine's maid, prior to which she was a young, formerly homeless (as she discloses), the relationship should not be read at face value. As Claudine's "thanks" to Zefa for the sexual services she provided her husband underscores, the situation should be read like nothing short of sexual exploitation. To those who may adopt this oppositional read-ing, Mitchell (2020) reminds us that in popular culture, the Mulatta figure has consistently been used to help justify her own exploitation as her hypersexu-ality has been traditionally framed as a need to be satisfied. Mitchell adds that in Brazil, the Mulatta represents racial, sexual, and gender excess. Although she is not marriage material, the Mulatta is readily available for sexual plea-sure and exploitation. Finally, Mitchell suggests that since telenovelas reflect and mediate the Brazilian imaginary, it is not surprising that they naturalize the sexual exploitation and economic marginalization of characters of African descent (p. 104).

In addition to her sexual exploitation, Zefa's narrative of having given her white son to be raised in a white world with all of its possibilities, while her Black son was raised in the kitchen with all of its limitations, remind us that the differential treatment of Black family members based on whether they have darker skin or lighter skin has real stakes for people's lives. Hordge-Freeman (2015) posits the idea of "affective capital," explaining that "positive emotions generated from affirming social interactions within and outside families can generate personal resources linked to greater creativity, resilience, and emotional well-being." However, Hordge-Freeman also points out that, due to the fact that love and affection can be distributed alongside racial lines, those family members who are phenotypically closer to Black may have experiences in their families that can be detrimental to their sense of self and their feelings of belonging (p. 5). For example, Hordge-Freeman (2015) observes that when real-life parents abandon their darker children or treat them worse than their lighter children, then for those children "unequal access to these positive emotions and experiences decreases self-confidence, increases personal insecurity, and engenders emotional boundaries that can hinder one's life" (p. 131). In both reality and the telenovela context, this type of racism also affects a Black person's ability to advance through life economically, limiting their class mobility, educational opportunities, and social status. In other words, it represents yet another previously unacknowledged form of racial inequality, as Gillam (2019, para 5) points out. In *Segundo Sol*, such pervasive anti-Black racism actually serves a narrative function, in that it helps to justify Roberval's villainous actions, which I will discuss in more detail in the following chapter.

Ultimately, all of the aforementioned situations and narrative devices show us how Zefa exemplifies the restrictive trajectory forced upon women of African descent in Brazil. This trajectory confines the personal development of Black women within a strict linearity: they progress from being Mulattas to becoming Mammies, all the while experiencing no economic or class mobility, and being subjected and subjugated to a life of racism and exploitation. As Gilliam & Gilliam (1995) suggest, millions of women in Brazil will be represented in more than one stage of this trajectory over their years, from being a sexualized Mulatta and thus objectified in youth, to being a nurturing and non-threatening woman when they are older (p. 530).

Zefa's character also serves to remind us that in the fantasy world of telenovelas, as in their real everyday lives, Afro-Brazilian women employed in domestic duties consider sexual abuse by the man of the house as one of the greatest risks in their profession. They are oftentimes victims of extortion at work, forced to choose between sexual submission and absolute poverty for themselves and their family. This is a lingering and systemic historical problem with its roots in slavery, as enslaved Black women suffered even more oppression than those "common" to Blacks. During slavery Black women were particularly exploited within a patriarchal society, working as maids (sometimes referred to as "Black milk mothers") and treated as sexual objects. In addition to these roles, enslaved Black women were valued and used for the reproductive capacities, which ensured the maintenance of the slave economy generation over generation, thereby preserving slavery as an institution (Da Silva, 2017, p. 30–32).

With this historical context in mind, we can understand Roberval as reminiscent of generations of "slave children" and in the continuation of an oppressive system: the inherit legacy of the majority of Afro-Descendants who still occupy the physical and/or, service role labor force in Brazil. In fact, in an ironic twist, in the same episode that Claudine and Zefa are having their heart to heart, Roberval actually mentions the *senzala* (slave quarters) in the next scene, when he is shown kissing the mixed-race cook Cacau, who is resisting his advances because she is "on the clock," to which he replies: "even Blacks in the *senzala* could love each other at the time of slavery." He therefore wonders, "why can't we?" (*Segundo Sol*, May 6, 2018).

In addition to the Jezebel, Mulatta, and Mammie stereotypes, Zefa also embodies another stock characteristic applied to Brazilian Black women in both telenovelas and society: that of the maid who has sex with her male employer. Because phenotypically Zefa's Black skin is relatively light—lighter in fact than her son Roberval's skin color—we can infer as part of Zefa's backstory that in her youth she likely would have been described as a Mulatta. According to Mitchell (2020), the Mulatta stereotype describes as a body that is (hyper) sexually available and that embodies phantasies of inter-racial desire while simultaneously manifesting racial hierarchies (pp. X, 4).

The Mulatta figure has a long history of being a part of Brazilian tele-novelas, which includes featuring in *Duas Caras,* ten years prior to *Segundo Sol*. Here, the character Sabrina portrays of the Afro-Brazilian woman who finds her way to her employer's "master" bedroom (pun intended). Sabrina was a maid at the household of the white protagonist, Julia Barreto, where she was having a sexual relationship with Julia's brother, Barretinho. This subplot sparked outrage when it first aired, as some audience members read this to mean that the maid was not only being sexually harassed, but also had succumbed to the white boss's advances in a "non-spoken type of racism" (p. 56–58). As Lobo & Orofino (2008) state, Barretinho is clearly harass-ing Sabrina, which is a situation reminiscent of the Brazilian slave heritage where in addition to performing daily maid duties, many enslaved women also served as vehicles of sexual gratification of their bosses, and the sexual initiation of their sons (Joyce, 2012, para 12–13).

In *Segundo Sol*, when Roberval confronts his mother Zefa about the fact that his white boss Severo is indeed his father, we can clearly see a number of tropes applied to Black women come to the fore. These include stereotypes of Black women as sexually exploitation, harassment, as sexy maids, as Mulattas, and even as Mammies. Roberval begins the confrontation by tell-ing Zefa that she "took away his right to have a father," and asks her if she thinks this is fair. He also asks "Why? Were you ashamed because you were laying with your boss, is that it? Are you still protecting Doctor Severo?" he asks[3]. Roberval concludes that "it would not look good for Severo if people knew he was laying with the maid." Zefa responds by begging her son to please forgive her, saying that she knows she "made a mistake, but I ask

you, please don't mention this to Dr. Severo." Roberval cannot believe his
mother's reaction and asks "why are you so afraid of this man? You spent
your life dedicated to him and his family." He also points out that as much as
Claudine wants to paint a picture of them all belonging to a happy mixed-race
family, this is not a family, but a complicated hierarchical power relationship
marked by race, class, and gender imbalance and oppression (*Segundo Sol*,
May 22, 2018).

Later in the same episode such themes come up again in another raw,
emotional discussion, showing once again that telenovelas are a complex
site of mediations that do not influence society in cannot be clearly placed
in a dichotomy of either entirely good or bad ways. In other words, the
same production can have pointed politicized racial discussions as well as
representations that are based on traditional racist stereotypes. This is also
a recurring characteristic of telenovelas, as pointed out by Joyce (2012) in
the analysis of *Duas Caras*. For example, the dialogue that takes place after
Claudine's funeral between Roberval and Severo Athayde is reminiscent of a
dinner party in *Duas Caras* which featured blatant racist dialogue and terms,
including the Brazilian equivalent of the N-word. The scene was fiction but
was able to effectively highlight actual racism in Brazilian society and in the
fictional televised one (Joyce, 2012, pp. 93–77).

The confrontation between Roberval and his white father takes place in
the den of the Athayde family home. It is a spacious and formal space, filled
with works of art on the walls, lush curtains, large windows, and expensive
looking furniture. Severo is sitting at a leather chair, in the corner of the room,
head in hands, immediately after Claudine's funeral. It is then that Roberval
walks into the room, defiantly, sitting behind his father/employer's desk.
Severo asks him what he thinks he is doing and tells him to "put himself in
his place." Roberval then reveals that Claudine told him the family's dirty
secret just before she died. He proceeds to push Severo a step further by placing his feet on top of Severo's desk, crossing his arms and leaning back. He
then asks: "What are you going to do, fire me, for being an insolent flunky?"
Severo replies that he should give Roberval a "beating with my belt," to
which Roberval responds that "now you are talking like a father." Although
Roberval is referring to the fact that "real" (i.e., biological, familial) fathers
discipline their children, the dialogue could also be read as reminiscent of
corporal punishment inflicted during the time of slavery, when white slave
owners beat enslaved people for disobedience if not with a belt then with a
whip (*Segundo Sol*, May 22, 2018).

As the scene escalates, the somber instrumental score becomes more prominent. Severo asks Roberval "how dare" he "speaks to him this way, after
he has just buried his wife." Roberval interrupts him saying "and yet, why
won't you fire me, daddy?" To the Brazilian audience, this question clearly

points to the fact that, according to Brazilian labor laws, if fired, Roberval would be legally entitled to walk away with all his worker's rights, such as a salary balance, prior notice, a severance package, and so on. At this point, Severo points his finger at him and demands that Roberval stop calling him "dad." Zefa then walks in the room and pleads with her son: "Stop this, he just buried his wife." Roberval mocks the situation, saying "poor Doctor Severo Athayde, poor guy. Your lover, my father" (*Segundo Sol*, May 22, 2018).

The scene ends with Roberval asking Severo if the reason why he should stop calling him dad is because Severo is worried that all he wants is the Athayde family's money. He adds that he does not want anything from him, that he is in fact ashamed of him and of his mother, and that if Severo does not fire him, he will quit and walk away with nothing. He finally says: "I quit, I do not want to stay here and you will as well, mother, let's leave this slave-driving family." Zefa pleads for him to stop. Roberval wonders what "this means," and questions if this is her way of asking him "to choose between your blood family and the Plantation Masters?" Zefa, the good old Mammie chooses to stay in her white master's house. Roberval tells her that by "choosing to stay here and to keep serving this family in every way possible," Zefa is effectively deciding to remain in her "slave quarters" (*Segundo Sol*, May 22, 2018).

This emotional and complex scene works on various levels. Like in the dinner scene in *Duas Caras*, the figure of the racist patriarch in *Segundo Sol* can be interpreted as an allegory of racism in Brazil more generally. For the purposes of the main analysis in this chapter, the text above is also noteworthy in that it again illustrates the two lingering representational stereotypes embodied by the character of Zefa: that of the Mammie who remains loyal to the family she served, and the Mulatta, who engaged in a sexual relationship with her employer and bore a son by him. as well as this very devastating fact: the historical sexual harassment and rape of Black women.

Yet there is another reading of this text that treats it as more progressive than it might initially appear. Namely, the racist dialogue, with references to slavery and its legacy, can also be understood as an attempt to ignite a conversation with viewers about race and representation not just within the plot of the telenovela, but in society more broadly (Joyce, 2012, p. 94). In this reading, Roberval's questioning and defiant nature reveal the telenovela as a site of struggle for representation and identity. Together, the representation of Black domestic workers in the two telenovelas discussed in this chapter, Sabrina (*Duas Caras*) and Zefa (*Segundo Sol*), reminds us that historically Afro-Brazilian women remain largely relegated to domestic work (Andrews, 1991, p. 69), with limited possibility for upward mobility and ample opportunity to be sexually harassed and exploited[4]—in real life and on TV.

Used in both *Duas Caras* and *Segundo Sol*, the strategy of using blatant dialogue to introduce ideas and discussions about racism is a lingering representational device. And while the dialogue can be read as controversial, as Joyce (2012) demonstrates, it can also be seen as a resourceful strategy. For example, actor Fabrício Boliveira, who played Roberval, gave an interview around the time *that Segundo Sol* aired in which he stated that he is highly favorable of such representation, claiming that he thinks it is important to have intelligent dialogue that audiences can engage with critically, and that these types of discussions are more important than discussing "who killed who," which is common in so many telenovela (Atrizes negras francesas, 2018, para 5–6).

Finally, the dialogue between Roberval, Severo, and Zefa, pointing to the story line involving two biological brothers that are phenotypically different and therefore constructed as racially different (white and Black), reminds us that although race is a social and not biological term, it has very real consequences in both the fictional telenovela world and the real world. As Sovik (2009) states, in the current debate about Brazilian racism, it is reiterated that racial difference has no biological basis, but in fact, lack of scientific basis turns out to be irrelevant. Sovik adds that in the search for new ways to analyze racial hierarchies, what matters is not the biological truth, but how much a statement can attract the support of its audience. The author considers that the falsehood of the inferiority of Blacks and Indigenous people is a peaceful point, in scientific terms; and also considers that the presumption of this view continues to operate on a daily basis. Finally, Sovik also reminds us that the biological fact that the same couple can have children identified as white and as Black does not negate racism in society (p. 17).

In fact, the "Black mother, white child" trope was not new to *Segundo Sol*, but is one that has been used in TV Globo telenovelas in the past. For example, in the 1997 telenovela *Por Amor* ("Anything for Love"), there was a story line involving an interracial couple and a marriage between a Black woman (Márcia) and a white man, Wilson. The latter character was played by a blond-haired, green-eyed actor. Although Wilson professed his love for his wife, he often expressed racism about possibly having Black offspring. In fact, he went so far as to not want to be a father based on the racist fear that his child would phenotypically *look* Black, and therefore in the eyes of Brazilian society (and his own eyes) *be* Black. In the end, however, Márcia ends up having a phenotypically white daughter. This, however, is also the source of much racism. For example, Márcia was identified as the child's nanny by other parents at the playground, which led to many discussions when the program aired about race and racism, and what it means to be Black or white in Brazil (Grijó & Sousa, p. 190).

While the story line of the phenotypically white and Black siblings may seem like a melodramatic plot device suitable only to telenovelas, it has also been used as a trope to reimagine race and racism in other media. But while in the telenovelas discussed in this chapter the plot device highlights racism, in journalism, for instance, it has been used for the opposite purpose: to actually erase racism. For example, on June 6, 2007, the Brazilian newsmagazine *Veja* featured a photo of 18-year-old identical twin brothers Alan and Alex Teixeira da Cunha on its cover, with the headline "Race does not exist." The headline meant to erase the existence of race altogether, since it was highlighting that one brother was considered white and the other Black, according to the Brazilian quota system. The racial distinction was based on phenotype, or how their skin appeared (Azevedo, 2007). Another current example can be seen on the cover of the April 2018 cover of *National Geographic,* where 11-year-old fraternal twins Marcia and Millie Biggs appear behind the headline "Black and white. These twin sisters make us rethink everything we know about race." Here, Marcia represents a white body, and Millie a Black one.

So, while the journalistic discourse seems to be one of a happy ending to racial difference, in *Segundo Sol* it works in the opposite way. As discussed, although the Mulatta stereotype can be applied to Zefa's younger years, as demonstrated above, the Mammie role is her key characteristic. In the Athayde household, she truly is the "mother of all."

MAMMIE ZEFA

The textual analysis in this section of the chapter will underscore Zefa's embodiment of the Mammie trope by offering additional examples from her interactions with other secondary characters in the narrative. For example, in one scene, Acácio, the boyfriend of Severo's adopted granddaughter, Manuela, brings her home in the middle of the night extremely high on drugs. He takes Manuela (who is white) to Zefa, not to her mother or father. Zefa is the one who bathes her, puts her in bed, kisses and caresses her face several times, and repeatedly calls her "my daughter, my love" while assuring "Manu" that "everything will be alright." Moments later, when Manu is in bed in her pajamas, she cries and tells Zefa that she is "her true mother," and begs Zefa to never treat her as her "boss" (*Segundo Sol*, /5/25/2018).

Zefa's Mammie role comes up again in a dialogue between Rochelle, Manuela's stepsister and Severo's biological granddaughter, and Zefa. Once again, this scene has an interesting dualistic nature: while we can read it as a traditional, stereotypical way to represent older Black women—Mammies— we can also read it as a way to question this very caricature. When the nature of Zefa's service role and lack of personal life is questioned by the character Rochelle, it allows the audience a moment to question this Brazilian reality of having a Black, *mestiza,* or Indigenous maid take care of the children of a wealthy white employer. Both a cinematographic trope and a relevant political question, this theme also features in recent films such as the Brazilian *The Second Mother* (2015) as well as in the Academy award winning *Roma* (2018) by Alfonso Cuarón, set in Mexico City.

In *Segundo Sol*, Rochelle defiantly tells Zefa that "she is a naïve old lady who knows nothing about life" since she "spent all her life in that house raising other people's kids." Rochelle adds that Zefa is like "an old piece of furniture." But Zefa defends herself, replying that Rochelle knows nothing about her "history and that she has lived a lot and is actually ashamed to see what a horrible person her little girl Rochelle has turned into." Even as Rochelle appears to be schooling Zefa about the reality of her oppressed life, the "good old Mammie" Zefa defends her "choices" and refers to Rochelle, her boss, as "my girl" and her own "family." While this dialogue shows that Zefa does have some agency to speak her mind and speak up to her boss, it also validates Rochelle's point that Zefa has spent her life raising other (white) people's children—two generations, in fact (*Segundo Sol*, May 25, 2018).

Another scene that depicts Zefa as Mammie involves a dialogue between Edgar (the white son) and his mother Zefa, moments after Roberval returns to his hometown as a mysterious rich man (in the contemporary plotline, twenty years later). Zefa had just met with him for the first time since he had left, and she had chosen to stay in the Athayde household. Edgar walks into the kitchen as she is cooking "his favorite meal ever since he was a child." He thanks her, saying that she "spoils him too much." He then says "come here," and gently kisses her forehead. Edgar thanks her for taking such good care of him, his daughters, and his father. Zefa tells "Mister Edgar" to stop that, claiming that she loves "working for all of you." Edgar replies: "'Mister'?' How many times have I told you that when we are alone you can feel free to call me just Edgar? You are practically part of the family." Zefa smiles back at him happily: "Okay, Ed-gar," slowly emphasizing his first name (*Segundo Sol*, May 25, 2018).

The dialogue above is exemplary of the Mammie role played by Zefa. While she has the responsibilities of childrearing, cooking, and cleaning, and has been exploited sexually, she is nonetheless content not only to be "practically" a part of the Athayde family, but to be "practically" a part of her actual family, as she is in fact Edgar's biological mother. The scene also reveals the traditional white appreciation given to Mammies in these types of productions, as Bogle (2001) describes. As the scene goes on, Edgar interrupts Zefa's happy giggles and says that he knows that her son Roberval has returned to town. Zefa is devastated by this comment and reveals to

Edgar that even though she was relieved to know that her son was alive and well after having disappeared for twenty years, she was also devastated, as Roberval told her that she is no longer his mother since she chose to stay at that house. At this moment, Edgar tries to console Zefa by holding her hands and telling her: "you are also my mother, my milk mother, the one who raised me." Edgar adds that Roberval will eventually forgive her, as he caresses her back and then kisses her forehead again. Zefa simply smiles and says, "may God listen to you" (*Segundo Sol*, June 2, 2018).

Zefa's extremely sweet nature and subordination was noticed in the popular press in an article analyzing the end of *Segundo Sol* and the characters that would not be missed by the general public. Such an article is customary practice in the country following the concluding episode of a telenovela. In it, the author writes that: "Zefa's tender subservience was deeply irritating. Working for a family that never had much respect for her, she preferred to serve the father of her two children, who never took her as a wife but only as a maid, than to live with her son, who wanted to give her a better life." The author adds that toward the end of the broadcast, Zefa left her submission aside "now at the end of the plot, but the damage was long done and she had already disappointed the public." In other words, it was "too little, too late" (Não vão deixar, 2018, para 8).

At this point, it is important to take into consideration that a key characteristic of telenovelas are their happy endings, along with the redemption of characters, who can go from evil to good, from spineless to daring, as in Zefa's case. The main criticism associated with this type of representation is that the audience spends several months with the weaker, more problematic representational version of the characters and then have maybe two weeks of a "comeback" that drives the "happy ending." This character development structure was also present in *Duas Caras*. As noted in *Brazilian Telenovelas and the Myth of Racial Democracy*, while that program served to ignite a metadiscourse of race and racism in Brazil (which can also be said of *Segundo Sol*), it also allowed for the traditional messages of telenovelas to go unchallenged, such as the formulaic happy ending, the eternal love triangles, and, of course, their consumerist messages. So, while Zefa may have redeemed her subservient modern-day-slave role at the end of the program, the key characteristics of the character, and the ones portrayed for the longest time (several months, on a daily basis), reinforced the stereotype of the sacrificial, passive, and oppressed but loving Mammie.

WHAT'S IN A NAME PART 1: ZEFA

I would like to conclude this analysis of Zefa by briefly note two additional issues with her portrayal that have historical precedents when it comes to representing Black people in Brazilian telenovelas. First, as Grijó & Souza (2012) point out, on the rare occasion that Blacks are represented in telenovelas, they are usually relegated to being slaves in "historical" productions, or domestic workers. A perhaps even more striking observation is the fact that even when Black characters are the protagonists in a telenovela, they are still relegated to service roles or secondary, low-paying jobs. For example, the previously discussed telenovela *Da Cor do Pecado*, the Black protagonist sold herbs. In *Cama de Gato*, the Black protagonist was a maid.

Finally, a notable, lingering characteristic of how Black characters are represented in Brazilian telenovelas is the fact that Blacks are almost always only identified by a first name or nickname, while whites almost always have a last name that features prominently in the narrative (Grijó & Sousa, 2012, pp. 193–194). As Joyce & Martinez (2019b) point out, Shakespeare's four-centuries-old question "What's in a name?" remains poignant, in texts about Blacks. The importance or lack of importance of references to a family name is relevant from a philosophical, social, and scientific point of view (p. 272). The fact that Black characters lack a proper family name is yet another tool of dehumanization, objectification, and oppression that should not go unnoticed.

CONCLUSION

As Mitchell (2020) states, telenovelas function as a crucial space for including Afro-Brazilians in the public sphere (p. 102). Thus, representation matters, and how groups are represented in telenovelas is a topic worthy of scholarly investigation. Most saliently, studying the topic helps us to understand identity formation, and the circulating discourses about race and racism in societies. This chapter took up that challenge through a careful examination of an Afro-Brazilian character: Zefa, the aging Black woman who lived and worked for the white Athayde family for most of her adult life.

The analysis revealed a peculiar characteristic in the portrayal of Zefa as simultaneously embodying two prominent, engrained stereotypes applied to the female Black body in visual media: that of the hypersexual and/or racially mixed woman (Jezebel, or Mulatta), and that of the sweet and sacrificial mother of all (Mammie). That portrayal was possible due to the fact that narratively *Segundo Sol* spanned a period of twenty years.

As a Mulatta, Zefa served to satisfy her white employer's sexual appetite, taking the sexual burden off of his white wife, who actually thanked her for it. In Stuart Hall's model, the relationship between Claudine and Zefa can be decoded as one of friendship, partnership, camaraderie, and love. They are depicted as consenting adults who entered into not only a love triangle, but through that triangle created a type of blended family, as Claudine raised one of Zefa's child as her own. However, a closer, more engaged reading of the story line opens up a more critical, oppositional reading, revealing racism, sexual harassment, and class, race, and gender oppression. As former Brazilian president Dilma Roussef pointed out, there was an important reason why her government's cash transfer policies focused on women: according to her, poverty in Brazil has a face—one that is Black and female (Dilma diz, November 19, 2011, para 1–2).

The analysis also revealed that Zefa's portrayal in *Segundo Sol* is akin to the maid Sabrina in *Duas Caras*: they were both young maids who were sexually harassed by their white bosses. However, while this was decoded as consensual, my analysis reveals that it should not be read as such. As both Black women were poor and employed by their sexual "partners," the situation should be read as sexual harassment, or even as rape. The story line is complicated further by the fact that Zefa "chooses" to give her white son to her barren female boss. This decision, in an historical context, points to Black women's role in the perpetuation of slavery by replenishing the enslaved workforce by supplying it with additional Black bodies. It also reveals one of the legacies of slavery in Brazil: its connection to class and the lack of class mobility, relegating Black and mixed bodies to service roles and/or those involving physical labor (in fact one of the reasons used for the implementation of affirmative action policies in the country). In the case of the telenovela, Roberval, the Black son, eventually becomes the family's driver.

Another stereotypical depiction traditionally used to represent the Black female Body was identified in Zefa's representation: Mammie. Specifically, this chapter revealed the many ways in which Zefa embodied the image of the subservient loving Mammie by examining scenes involving multiple characters that she lovingly "mothered": Roberval, Edgar, Severo, Claudine, Manuela, and Rochelle. Some of the production devices used to highlight this representation were storylines, soft background music, camera close-ups, and, especially, dialogue.

Yet while this investigation revealed that *Segundo Sol*, like other telenovelas, relied heavily on stereotypes, it also highlighted the fact that frank, poignant, political, and sometimes racist dialogue can simultaneously serve as a powerful tool in igniting discussion about race and racism in society. In this sense, dialogues involving race in *Segundo Sol* were reminiscent of those in

Duas Caras, which highlighted and spurred questions about matters of race and racism in Brazil.

The analysis also pointed out that on the rare occasions where Brazilian telenovelas have depicted Black characters, these characters are usually only referred to by their first name, while the majority of white characters have family names that are repeated throughout the narrative. This lends the white characters importance and humanity. It also has connotations related to these white characters as belonging to traditional nuclear family, something not awarded to Black bodies. Additionally, a more salient observation is the fact that even when they are protagonists, Black characters are still relegated to service or slave roles (Grijó & Souza (2012, pp. 193–194).

As Stuart Hall (1995) reminds us, what the media produce is, precisely, representations of the social world—images, descriptions, explanations, and frames for understanding how the world is and why it works as it is said and shown to work. Furthermore, amongst other kinds of ideological labor, the media construct for us a definition of what race is, what meaning the imagery of race carries, and what the "problem of race" is understood to be. They help to classify the world in terms of the categories of race (p. 20). This chapter's analysis of the character Zefa is a step in this direction.

While Zefa's representation can be said to be stereotypical, we cannot underscore that most of her dialogue with her son Roberval as highlighting deep and ingrained notions of race and racism in Brazilian society. This has been a characteristic of Globo telenovelas that have addressed race matters since *Duas Caras* aired in 2008. In fact, as Nunes (2019) reminds us, due to the nature of the themes in that program, the traditional "8 o'clock" prime-time telenovela had to be moved to the nine pm timeslot, a stipulation from the Justice Ministry which classified the program as inappropriate for viewers under fourteen due to its blatant racially charged dialogues and situations. The term "8 o'clock" telenovela, which had been traditionally used to classify those programs airing immediately after the National News, was officially changed in 2011 to "9 o'clock telenovela" (*Novela das 9*, p. 3).

Finally, this chapter has reminded us that telenovelas are a very lucrative commercial product that cannot be regarded as just that—a vehicle for selling goods. As García Canclini (2001) reminds us, consumption can be empowering. As the Latin American Cultural Studies tradition highlights, viewers should look beyond the manipulative and commercial role of the media to simply sell us things such as manufactured goods. The examination above is pragmatic in the sense that it understands that while telenovelas are texts produced by a globally powerful commercial network aimed at making money, these texts can also create dialogue and generate ("sell") ideas that may meaningfully contribute to social justice.

NOTES

1. Just to clarify once again, Edgar is Zefa's white-skin son with her employer Severo, who is Claudine's husband.

2. I am using the expression "white-passing" here freely and for context, as in Brazil, phenotype is the actual determinant of race, as discussed previously. Therefore, in the telenovela as in real life, Edgar is effectively white, as he *looks* white. Roberval is effectively Black, as he *looks* Black.

3. Calling someone a "Doctor" in Brazil is a sign of social class hierarchy and respect and signifies the individual's high social class. Even though a person may not in fact be a doctor, calling them one signifies that they have money and power.

4. I should note that in Brazil, domestic work was only protected under worker's rights and labor protection legislation starting in 2013 with the Constitutional Amendment 72 (CA 72), which expanded the rights of domestic workers, and of the Enabling Law (LC) 150 of June 1st, 2015, which brought most of these rights into effect.

Chapter Three

His Body

*Slaves, Bucks, Villains, and N*gg@s*

This chapter will examine the representation of two Black male characters in *Segundo Sol*: Roberval, the Black villain, and Acácio, Manuela's boyfriend (also briefly discussed in the previous chapter). In productions as large as telenovelas, with dozens of characters, there is always room for more than one "villain" and more than one "hero," hence the qualifier "Black" villain applied to Roberval. The close textual analysis of these Black male characters aims to shed light on the representation of Blacks in Brazilian telenovelas more broadly. As we will see, the portrayals of Roberval and Acácio point to a few lingering representational stereotypes, but also open up possibilities for introducing novel ideas and topics that can contribute to a broader discussion about race and racism in contemporary Brazil.

As previously discussed, the plotlines of *Segundo Sol* take place in two separate temporalities: the first couple of weeks of the broadcast are set "in the past" (the year 2000), and episodes during the following months are set in the present (2018), though are interspersed with some flashbacks from twenty years earlier. In the first two weeks of the program, Roberval is the Black bastard son of Zefa and Severo Athayde and serves as the Athayde family's driver. In the subsequent months set decades later, he is an extremely rich man in his mid-to late thirties. He is also seeking revenge against his racist father. Acácio, who is only in the "present" time of the program (2018) is a young Black man in his early twenties. He is a medical student, although he was rarely seen on campus or going to school, and certainly never at a hospital or clinic. Acácio is usually seen playing *Capoeira*, the Brazilian martial art born as part of a resistance to slavery, as well as in his place of residence, the *Casarão* ("The Big House"), an illegally occupied house where he has started a utopian Black community where no one pays rent, but all contribute to the wellbeing of its members by cooking, cleaning, childrearing, and performing other tasks. While this chapter provides a close textual analysis of the representation of Roberval and Acácio in *Segundo Sol,* we can identify parallels to Evilásio's representation in the *Duas Caras,* the first primetime telenovela to present audiences with a Black hero.

It is important to note that as in *Duas Caras*, the representation of Black characters in *Segundo Sol* is complex and cannot be easily described as either completely "good" or completely "bad." On one hand, the representation of Black bodies in the program relied heavily on traditional negative stereotypes. On the other hand, it also stands to show how telenovelas serve as a vehicle that help open up discussions about race in Brazil. Starting from the initial controversy due to the lack of Black actors in the promo, the telenovela evolved to present audiences with a plot filled with racially charged dialogues questioning the lingering effects of slavery in the country. As Fabrício Boliveira (the actor who plays Roberval) noticed, the public's reaction to the perceived racism in *Segundo Sol* even before the program started was a "true sign of the times." He added that TV Globo painted Bahia in such a way that the population noticed that the portrayal did not match reality and was vocal about it, and that the incident actually helped spark a series of discussions about racism in the country (Barros 2018a, para 2).

Boliveira also discussed the importance of having race matters represented in telenovelas, pointing out that there is a lack of central roles for Blacks in Brazilian TV as well as films, and that these casting discrepancies are actually "a question of the country's identity." Additionally, the actor credits the Black movement and activism in Brazil for pushing such discussions and points out that TV programs need to be open to such conversations and include them in their dialogue. Boliveira reminds us that this is part of a larger discussion, commenting that in the United States, "even the Oscars is talking about representativeness, then why is Brazil, a country made up mostly of Blacks, going to be left behind?" (Barros 2018a, para 2).

Considered holistically, the representation of Blacks in *Segundo Sol* is largely akin to the representations in *Duas Caras*. In the latter production, Evilásio was a groundbreaking character who represented an important shift in the representation of Afro-Brazilians, especially males: he was the first main Black "hero" of a nine o'clock telenovela, whose overall positive portrayal marked a step toward the greater inclusion of Blacks in the telenovela genre. However, that representation was nonetheless contradictory, as he was also characterized as a hypersexualized Black man, which Bogle (2001) described as "Buck." For instance, he was often seen shirtless, in sexual situations with multiple white partners, and with women gazing at his body and lusting over him.

The examination of both Roberval and Acácio from *Segundo Sol* reveals that the hypersexualized Black man is a lingering trope used to represent

Black bodies in TV Globo telenovelas. For example, Roberval is portrayed as virile hypersexual male who satisfies a plethora of women ranging in age, marital status, race, and class. Thus, at first glance, Roberval's representation reveals the ongoing problematic ways in which Black men have been portrayed in Brazilian telenovelas. Like Zefa, who embodied two distinctive stereotypes (Jezebel and Mammie), Roberval too embodies an intersectional gender and race-based representational trope: villain and virile.

However, as this chapter will show, a textual analysis of Roberval's dialogues about race and racism reveals a more complex and nuanced character portrayal. Although Roberval's representation can be seen at times as problematic, we must note that it does have some positive aspects as well. As Benício (2018) notes, that character goes beyond the Black-supporting role and acts to deflate the accusations received by TV Globo that they were racists and completely ignoring Blackness in Bahia. Benício further states that, in fact, Roberval is a valuable presence in the plot, above what is normally seen in Globo's prime time productions and adds that Roberval can be considered the second male protagonist, behind singer Beto Falcão, the white protagonist (para 4–6).

ROBERVAL

As Grijó & Souza (2012) point out, the Black-as-villain trope in Brazilian telenovelas can be identified as early as 1976, with its most famous iteration being that of the slave Rosa in the telenovela *Escrava Isaura* / "Slave Girl Isaura." In the following years, while some Black characters were represented as cordial and friendly (akin to Bogle's (2001) Toms and Mammies), most were portrayed as robbers, murderers, and service workers. Later, in the first decade of the 2000s, the Black villain trope comes back in full force. For example, in the telenovela *A Favorita* / "The Favorite" (2008), Grijó & Souza write that we see the Black villain with "the most repercussion" in that entire decade. Namely, they analyze Romildo Rosa, a rich man and politician who owned his own (very large) home and was the first Black family man to occupy the world of the rich upper class in Brazilian telenovelas. He also had, as the authors point out, a prominent family name. However, he was extremely unethical and was involved in the trafficking of arms and all sorts of shenanigans (p. 199). However, we must note that, as is customary in telenovelas, the character does redeem himself toward the end of the plot, complicating the notion of villainy.

The question of whether Roberval is a "true" villain is an interesting one. As Fabrício Boliveira (the actor who played Roberval) points out, Roberval is a complex, multilayered character who is traumatized. This complexity strays from the unidimensional stereotypes often used to depict Blacks in telenovelas. According to Boliveira, Roberval's "actions are incorrect, but at the same time his goals seem to be correct. He enters this space of duality and non-Manichaeism, one of non-hero, non-villain."[1] The actor adds that what he "strived for and achieved with this role was to open up discussions and to ask questions," which he in fact witnessed in public discussions and in the media, including social media. Boliveira further states that "this is the role of art: to not just give one answer, but to discuss and to clash." The actor concludes that "for me this is the great victory of this character" (Santana, 2018, para 13–16).

The other main race-based trope that Roberval embodies in his seemingly boundless sexual appetite, strong sexual appeal and inclining to breaking the law, is that of the Black Buck. Throughout the telenovela, Roberval had sexual relations with several white women, even working as a prostitute for the white villain Laureta, the owner of a high-class brothel. Thus, like Evilásio's character in *Duas Caras,* Roberval can be described as conforming to Bogle's (2001) characterization of the "Buck." Adding to this stereotypical representation is the fact that, production wise, Roberval's body is cut up into pieces through strategic close ups: abs, biceps, lips. As far as dialogue, several of Roberval's white sexual partners refer to him as being "insatiable," the "best lover they have ever had"; and "I want to be yours" throughout the narrative. In this sense, both Evilásio and Roberval (and Acácio, as I will demonstrate below) can also be said to be depicting the traditional "Black other" as described by bell hooks (1992): a sex symbol whose body is ready to be "eaten" and consumed by white women.

A careful reading of the representational journey taken by Roberval, one that spanned two decades, offers a deeper understanding of the current nature of representation of Blacks in Brazil, as well as surrounding discourses. As previously discussed, after two decades living in Africa, Roberval comes back to Brazil as a successful, rich man. The audience later finds out that he is involved in the illegal diamond trade in Africa despite posing as a Brazilian real estate mogul in Brazil. He returns to Brazil to take revenge on his racist father with a grand plan: take away all his money, expose his wrongdoings, humiliate him, and ultimately overpower him. This transformation is observed in the narrative, as well as in production elements surrounding the character, such as his costuming. For example, in spite of the extreme heat in Bahia, when he is dressed, Roberval often wears well-tailored suits with buttoned-up shirts and ties. The suits are usually dark grey or black, another trope of villainy. He no longer wears braids in his hair as he had when he was living with the Athayde's performing his role as the family driver, but now has his hair cut short. It is interesting to note that in the beginning of the broadcast, Roberval's braids were praised by critics as a good representational device and were highlighted in the press as a symbol of Black power/empowerment, as well as Black consciousness in Brazil (Benício, 2018, para 5).

The first character Roberval meets upon returning to Brazil after two decades in Africa is his lost love, Cacau, who is the white protagonist's sister. He takes her out to a fancy dinner and gives her a diamond necklace as a gift. But when Cacau mentions Roberval's mother Zefa, Roberval gets mad and asks her not to mention "that woman." He adds that Cacau knows that ever since his mom chose to stay with the family that "enslaves her in that big house," he has considered himself to be motherless, and in fact to be an orphan. Being a telenovela, of course, one of the first thing Cacau does after reuniting with Roberval is to tell Zefa where to find him (May 29, 2018).

Thus, by the third week of the broadcast, Roberval's role in the telenovela has been clearly defined: he is the (sexy) Black villain. But as is customary in telenovelas, this initial portrayal does not mean that he will remain evil throughout the program. Not only will Roberval perform random acts of heroism and kindness as the telenovela continues, but he will also have a chance to redeem himself at the end of the narrative. It is important to note that the audience knows his narrative arc from the outset. He is the villain who came back for revenge against his parents, but more specifically, his white racist father. He will have a chance to redeem himself at the end, but not without making his enemies suffer at great length first.

As Roberval begins to enact his plan to publicly humiliate Severo and to bring him to ruin, his mother visits him and says she cannot believe the things Roberval is doing to him. Roberval immediately replies: "Do you mean your former lover, or current one, who knows?" Zefa replies that this is "your family" and that "Severo is your father." Roberval then yells: "Oh now he is my father? And what family? I am not a part of that family and neither are you. Unless you have left the maid's quarters and are now sleeping in the master bedroom. But judging by your clothes you have not, you have not become first lady." Zefa begs her son to respect her as she is his mother, but he replies that he does not have respect for a mother who never fought for her son's birthrights, for the woman who opted to be a family's slave instead of his true mother. Once again, the dialogue between Roberval and Zefa is questioning ingrained racial problems that are central in the plot as well as in the broader Brazilian in society: above all, Roberval highlights Zefa's exploitation and subjugation by her employers (as previously discussed in chapter 2), which she still refuses to see (*Segundo Sol*, June 11, 2018).

As the scene progresses, such themes are further discussed as Zefa defends herself to Roberval by telling him that he does not know anything about her history of having been homeless and hungry, and that Severo's family brought her into their house and gave her shelter and a job, which pulled her out of poverty and starvation. Zefa insists that the Athaydes are a good family that allowed a single mother like her to raise him in their home, and also paid for his education. But Roberval quickly points out the class and racial chiasm that exists between them: *"Their* house. At one moment I am part of the family, then, they did me a favor? A job is not a favor. Do you feel indebted to him after having served him in bed, table, and bathroom?" he asks. Zefa replies that she is grateful and proud of working there, as the Athaydes are the only family she has ever known. Roberval finally says that the family will soon be in ruins and will fire her, but she can work for him as a cook to whom he will pay a proper salary. Zefa finally leaves, but not before calling him "a monster" (*Segundo Sol*, June 11/2018).

While the dialogue above may seem cruel, it can be said to aid in broader discussions about Brazil's racial reality. and while at times problematic, Roberval and Zefa's role play a key part in this process. As the actor Fabrício Boliveira (aka Roberval) points out in an interview with one the country's most traditional magazines, *Veja,* central roles for Blacks in film and television are lacking in Brazil. He states that: "It is a matter of the country's identity. The Black movement is growing, people are more prepared to have this discussion and works of art need to be open to this type of dialogue. "He adds that he hopes to contribute to the discussion of racism in the country as a whole and points out that "Roberval directly discusses the servile condition of Black people in this country, one that is addicted to slavery." He adds that Roberval's situation, "from the father who abandoned him and the mother who chose for his white brother to live in comfort, and left him in that servile job because of his color, incite this discussion" (Barros 2018b, para. 4–5).

Finally, in terms of Roberval's representation as "sexy Black villain," as with Romildo Rosa (in *A Favorita*). Roberval's "success" as a wealthy man is associated with crime, as it is revealed that his fortune stems from trafficking diamonds in Africa. In other words, he represents the traditional "outlaw" historically associated with the portrayal of Blacks in Brazilian telenovelas.

ACÁCIO

Acácio is another interesting character for analysis as he represents a different type of duality: while he is sexually hyperactive—the stereotype usually associated with "Buck"—he is also a good natured and hopeless romantic. Specialized media describe him as a "Black handsome man in his twenties, possessing good character. A *capoeirista*, (person who practices *capoeira*) who teaches *capoeira* at an academy in Santo Antônio, and studies medicine at a nearby college." A parallel can be drawn between Acácio and Evilásio from *Duas Caras* not only in terms of their hypersexual depiction, but also because they are each coupled with the young white female lead and face daily dosages of racism and classism. As his character description states, "he is one of the original founders of an occupation in an abandoned house where he became a kind of informal leader. He is in love with Manuela, who he has been dating for just over two years. The romance between Edgar's adopted daughter and a Black slum dweller is a source of embarrassment to the family, exposing racism in that house" (Vieira 2018a, para 2). The analysis of Acácio's representation coupled with the previously mentioned ones will give us a glimpse into how Blacks have been and continue to be represented in telenovelas. I must remind the reader that there were only five Black characters with recurring roles and lines in this program and that most of the other ones were merely "extras." Finally, the investigation will also serve to show how the telenovela text can spark conversations about race and racism in Brazil.

The first time the audience is introduced to the character of Acácio, he is engaged in a typical telenovela "make-out session" with his girlfriend Manuela (aka Manu). They are kissing and talking like young love birds. The backdrop is the ocean; and the couple is by a ledge overlooking it. Acácio is shirtless for no particular reason and the camera focuses on his body and muscular physique. This is the first time the audience hears him speak, as we are introduced to him through Manuela's point of view, and through the camera's fragmentation of his body. Manuela states that "My boyfriend is the best *capoeirista* in all of Bahia. It looks like you can fly away from the *roda*."[2] He replies that he would only "fly away straight into her arms." Manuela tells him that she pities the other players, as Acácio smiles and changes the subject: "Your birthday is coming soon, what are you going to do?" Manuela replies that her family is having a fancy dinner at her house and asks him if he wants to come. Acácio replies that "It's about time I meet your family" (*Segundo Sol*, May 24, 2018).

For audiences familiar with American cinema, the story line is reminiscent of the classic movie *Guess Who Is Coming to Dinner* (1967), in which a wealthy white women brings home her African American boyfriend to meet her conservative (and in many ways racist) parents. Intertextually, we can refer back to the iconic scene in *Duas Caras* where Julia, the wealthy white protagonist, brings her poor and Black boyfriend Evilásio to a family dinner, only to have her father call him a "cocky crioulo," an extremely racist expression akin to the *N word* in English. Adding to Evilásio's dehumanization, Julia's father and is also dehumanized when her dad wonders if Evilásio is indeed a person or if he should be referred to as "it" instead of "he" (Joyce, 2012, p. 94).

As the days go by in *Segundo Sol*, it is finally the day of Manuela's birthday, and Acácio arrives at the party. Once there, Manuela's adopted sister Rochelle Athayde tricks him into looking like he is a waiter by asking him to help her rearrange some wine glasses and to move a table. The audience can see through her facial expressions—she asks him this just as her family is approaching—that she is up to her evil ways. It is also implied that Rochelle knows her racist family and that due to the fact that he is Black, they will therefore assume he is a worker, not a guest. In this assumption, Rochelle was correct. As Manu's mother approaches them along with her husband Edgar and Severo, she is rude and condescending toward Acácio, telling him she will contact his boss and let him know what a poor job he is doing. She is backed by the Athayde family who all verbally express agreement with her. Manu walks in at this very moment and asks why they are being rude to her boyfriend. They apologize for the "mix up." Manu defiantly asks why they would naturally assume that Acácio was a waiter, implying that the reason must be because he is Black. At this moment, Acácio calmly intervenes by telling Manu that it was just because he was moving the table and some glasses around—that is, performing typical waiter duties (*Segundo Sol*, May 24, 2018).

As we can see, since the beginning of the broadcast Acácio was portrayed as good, sexy, handsome, romantic, and good natured, as well as a caring boyfriend to his girlfriend, the drug-addicted, Manu. This characterization continues throughout the program. For example, in the episode that aired on May 25, 2018, he "tricks" a very drunk/high Manu into leaving party by saying he is taking her to another party, when in fact he is taking her home. Moreover, he is actually bringing her to Mammie Zefa, who takes care of Manu by giving her a shower and putting her to bed. Right before Acácio leaves her home, Manuela shouts that he is a "very bad boyfriend" for bringing her home to be cared for, instead of to a party, where she could have gotten more drugs. Acácio simply replies "go to sleep, my love" and leaves.

In addition to being a caring boyfriend, Acácio is also portrayed as extremely loyal, wise, good natured, and a true leader in his community, the *Casarão*. For example, he explains to Manuela (and the audience) that he and his friends live in a community where members vote before making any decisions that affect the collective, and where all religions are welcome. As they walk into the house, Acácio shows Manuela (and the viewers) an altar that was created by members of the *Casarão* and adds that while they love to celebrate and have parties, drugs are not allowed in the house. As he walks her through every room in the colorful house, he explains that everything is shared: rooms, bathrooms, food, and cooking and cleaning duties. He also shows her the shower—a communal outdoor space on the rooftop (*Segundo Sol*, May 26, 2018).

Acácio can be read as both a happy leader and a tour guide that walks Manuela and viewers through his physical living quarters, a space that also serves as to underscore his good nature and upright character, as well as his position as leader and community organizer. This is problematic because it removes any obligation that the state has to its citizens as far as welfare, and basic human rights. For example, when Manuela asks Acácio what happens on a rainy day and they have to use the shower located on a rooftop without walls or a ceiling, Acácio smiles and simply replies that they shower anyway and share the space. The entire sequence also contributes to Acácio's duality between the extremely good natured and honest man, and the one who breaks the law by illegally living in a house that does not belong to him, sees nothing wrong with it, and seems quite happy and content about his living situation. While the space clearly lacks basic sanitation, as well as paint on the little walls that are still standing, and is in a state of physical disrepair, the *Casarão* is represented as upbeat and cozy, with colorful African inspired cloths used as room dividers. Because this is a Black community, the *Casarão* can be read as another way of subjugating "others," as its residents are depicted as being happy with no amenities—including basic sanitation and legal electricity—thus in some ways absolving the state of its responsibility to meet the basic welfare needs of its (Black) citizens (*Segundo Sol*, May 26, 2018).

Thus, while on one hand the *Casarão* is clearly encoded as an illegal occupation, on the other, everyone seems happy with their situation in this utopian community. Something else that is made clear in its depiction is the direct association between poverty and race: all of its residents are Black and supposedly do not "need" much to live. As Acácio and Manuela walk into Acácio's room, we see a mattress on the floor, prompting Manuela to ask, "if I live here, this is where we will sleep, in this hard mattress on the floor?" Acácio replies that a hard mattress would be the least of her problems, since they do not have proper electricity or running water. He follows this matter-of-fact remark by giving Manuela a passionate kiss on her lips. At this moment, however, the couple is suddenly interrupted by a small child of about five years of age, who comes in the room playing with a ball. When Manuela asks who he is, Acácio replies that it his "our" son, Tupã.[3] Manuela says she is confused, to which Acácio explains that although Tupã's blood mother is Renatinha, all of the women who live in the house consider themselves to be the child's mother, and all of the men in the house consider themselves his father. Minutes later, the three of them walk outside to share a communal meal. Here, Acácio's ex-girlfriend, a Black woman named Ludi, comments that Manuela is Acácio's "new whitey" (*Segundo Sol*, May 26, 2018). This expression was also used in *Duas Caras* ten years earlier when the protagonist Evilásio made love to his white girlfriend Julia; he referred to her as "my little whitey," and she called him "my big, delicious, negro" (Joyce, 2012, p. 62).

As we can see, in spite of the controversy surrounding the lack of Black representation in the promo for *Segundo Sol*, TV Globo did incorporate story lines highlighting race and racism in the narrative. Indirectly, the program also drew attention to the association between race and class. The fact that Acácio brings a "whitey" to live in the *Casarão* community does not sit well with some of the residents. For example, Ludi comments that Manuela is a "bored bougie," and that if Acácio brings home every white girl that sees him play *capoeira*, there would not be any room left in the house for the current residents. She then mentions Rochelle, Manuela's sister, who had come to see him play that same morning. Manuela storms out of the *Casarão* and heads directly to the Athayde home where, in front of her whole family, she asks Rochelle why she is flirting with her boyfriend. Rochelle belittles her sister's accusations and defends herself by replying that Manuela "is crazy," as she would never try to hook up with a "Black man." After Manuela leaves the room, the patriarch Severo dismisses the whole controversy by siding with Rochelle and wondering if Manuela might have been on drugs. Here we see another blatant stereotype: Rochelle replies that Manuela is probably on drugs since her boyfriend is not only Black, but also a *capoeirista,* and therefore likely a drug dealer (*Segundo Sol*, May 27, 2018).

While the situation above involves blatantly racist tropes, it is also ironic and was used to spark discussions about racism. As Vieira (2018a) states, "Manuela's white and rich family celebrate when she leaves Acácio for Narciso, a young white man from a 'good family' (meaning a white family). But they don't know that the new playboy boyfriend is a young delinquent who is going to plunge Manuela even further into drugs. But Acácio will never give up on Manuela and will try to save her" (Vieira 2018a, para 3).

While Acácio's portrayal as a good and loyal boyfriend remained unchanged throughout the broadcast—which was largely a positive portrayal for a Black character in a telenovela—the focus on his physique, body, and sexual appeal was also a constant, and a marker of his otherness. For example, in the episode that aired on May 25, 2018, Rochelle goes to the *Capoeira Roda* where Acácio is playing, and is seen lusting after him, gazing at different parts of his body and taking photos of him with her phone. The scene is produced in what can be described as a reversal of Laura Mulvey's (1975) male gaze, as here the audience stands in for Rochelle's gaze, and there is an exchange of viewpoints between the audience looking at Rochelle, who is looking/lusting at Acácio's body, and the audience standing in for her gaze. Production wise, and as far as the narrative. narrative Acácio's body is dissected into parts as the camera focuses on his physique, his muscles, his shirtless body, his agility, and virility (*Segundo Sol*, May 25, 2018).

Indeed, while Acácio is in his (Black) space—a capoeira *roda* surrounded by his friends—and should command his environment, it is clear that Rochelle is the one whose subjecthood and subjectivity is in control. The camera objectifies Acácio into serving as the subject of Rochelle's sexual desire and encodes in his fragmented body a characteristic described by Mulvey as "to-be-looked-at-ness," which disempowers the subject of the look while empowering the active gaze of the one who is looking. Thus, there is the double objectification of the Black body on and off screen: the objectification of Acácio's body within the narrative, and that of the Dan Ferreira's body—the actor who plays him—for those watching at home (*Segundo Sol*, May 25, 2018).

This theme of objectification of the Black body continues when Acácio walks by Rochelle, shirtless, and she looks him up and down, clearly eroticizing and objectifying his body. This goes even further when camera shots equate and fuse Acácio's body to nature, in a type of primitive oneness that renders him as an exotic part of the natural scenery and miscensene: one filled with Bahia's natural world, but also with the diegetic sounds of African drums, in addition to clapping, singing, and the practice of *capoeira*. It is against this backdrop that Rochelle states: "looking at you with your friends and the ocean behind you, I just had to take photos of you," and adds that "he looks like a model," while looking at him up and down, and adds that he could be on the cover of one of those "foreign magazines, shirtless," as she leans closer to him. Acácio is surprised that she is flirting with him and says he never thought he was Rochelle's type. She replies that she is "very interested" in him and that, besides being "handsome, he smells good and is all *gostoso.*" The scene is problematic in various ways: *gostoso* is an expression that literally means "yummy," and is usually associated with food. However, it also connotes sexiness in Brazil. When Rochelle tells Acácio he smells good while looking at his sweaty and shirtless body, we can read this as: she in effect encoding a primitive, natural characteristic onto his Black body, which makes him both irresistible to her but also "others" him. Rochelle adds that Acácio looks like he is "good at sex" (*Segundo Sol*, May 25, 2018).

As the scene progresses, Rochelle tells Acácio she laments the fact that he is seeing her sister, the "ugly Manuela." Acácio respond by telling Rochelle that she is not "even worth the clothes on her back," instructing her to go away. She says that she knows he is attracted to her, and that the attraction is "stronger than his will." And as she caresses the sweat that is dripping from his chest, she adds that the attraction is something is "not rational." Again, an extremely problematic statement referring to the young Black (man) as in Boggle's (1973) description of Bucks. She finally says: "it will happen in no time, *delicious*," as she blows him a kiss and walks away.

This equating of Acácio's body to food calls to mind bell hooks' (1992) theory of the "commodification of otherness." It is worthwhile to pause here and note that several Black *capoeiristas* can be seen in the background of the above scene—most of them older and heavier, some of them with a pronounced belly. This contrast serves to make Acácio's vitality and fit physical body stand out even more (*Segundo Sol*, May 25, 2018). Additionally, the scene can be described as what bell hooks (1992) refers to as "eating the other," as Acácio's Black body's oneness with nature, his sweat and irresistible smell, and the references that equate his body to food are evoked like an ethnic and racial commodity. As hooks writes, "within commodity culture, ethnicity becomes a spice, a seasoning that can liven up the dull dish that is mainstream white culture (hooks, 1992, p. 21).

The scene above is akin to a scene in *DuasCaras* in which Julia lusts after Evilásio while he is taking a shower with a hose on a rooftop. Most significantly, the same production elements were used in both scenes: cutting him up into individual parts of the male body, traveling up and down his wet chest, shoulders, and back, jumping back and forth between shots of the female character's gaze and the objectified Black male body. The similarities enable us to observe a lingering way in which young Brazilian Black bodies have been encoded in telenovelas, which is a prime example of hook's (1992) "commodification of others": "a delight, more intense, more satisfying than normal ways of doing and feeling" (p. 21). Such depictions also reflect what hooks deems the search for the ultimate individual pleasure, one so intense that the person experiencing it might not recover from it. hooks notes that it is precisely a longing for this pleasure that has led the predominantly white western world to sustain a romantic fantasy of and with the "primitive" through a Black body (the dark flesh) or a foreign country (hooks, 1992, p. 27).

Acácio's sexual nature and appetite are highlighted in other scenes as well. For example, he fulfills Rochelle's prophecy that he would eventually subdue to her charms and have sex with her despite being his girlfriend's half-sister; it was indeed an impulse stronger than his rational will, as Rochelle predicted. Thus, on the July 4th episode, Acácio has sex with Rochelle and tells her in bed afterwards: "I lived to see this: Rochelle Athayde, all beautiful, sweet smelling, lying completely naked, in a poor occupied house, on a mattress without a sheet, nor a pillow!" (Rodrigues, 2018, para 2).

A few episodes later, the audience is once again remined of Acácio's hyper sexuality in a scene that received significant media attention for exploring a largely taboo subject in Brazil: a threesome. The scene follows a fight between Acácio and Manuela and it features Acácio in bed having sex with not one but two young women who are residents of the *Casarão*, Renatinha and Ludi (his ex-girlfriend). While in bed, Renatinha asks Acácio: "If you had to choose between one of us, who would you choose, Acácio?" He replies: "What's with this crazy talk? I would choose not to choose and to be free." Ludi then joins in the conversation: "He would drop the two of us and go back to that rich spoiled girl Manuela in an instant." At this point, Renatinha states that "The problem is that Manuela never agreed to share you (Acácio) with us, she doesn't like our free love thing, without commitment!" (Novela Segundo Sol, 2018, paras 2–3). The conversation continues, and toward the end of scene Ludi tells Acácio that "Manuela is a square bougie. You (Acácio) are cooler without her."

Acácio is controversial in the same way that Evilásio was controversial: while his assumed sexual prowess is exploited over and over, he is also portrayed as a decent person in some contexts, your go to "good guy." For example, while Acácio informs Ludi and Renatinha that what they have is "pure sex," he clarifies that what he has with Manuela is "special and their own thing" (Novela Segundo Sol, 2018, paras 2–3). Again, we should point out that his young Black body is again represented as not only hypersexual, but this dialogue points to another exampling of "othering," as it reveals Acácio to be a wild and free Black man that breaks all the rules when with Black women, but a gentle hopeless romantic when with his white girlfriend Manu—which does not nullify his hyper sexual "condition." As hooks (1992) states

> Mass culture is the contemporary location that both publicly declares and per-petuates the idea that there is pleasure to be found in the acknowledgment and enjoyment of racial difference (. . .). Cultural taboos around sexuality and desire are transgressed and made explicit as the media bombards folks with a message of difference no longer based on the white supremacist assumption that "blondes have more fun." The "real fun" is to be had by bringing to the surface all those "nasty" unconscious fantasies and longings about contact with the Other embed-ded in the secret (not so secret) deep structure of white supremacy (pp. 12–22).

As the above scenes have indicated, most of the storylines associated with Acácio revolved around sex and break ups, and then break-up-sex. Thus, as observed in the popular press, "after just a few months, Acácio's stories vanished, and he ended up without any function within the telenovela. His coupling with Manuela ended up not captivating the audiences and without a story line to call his own, the character ended up making fewer and fewer appearances in the broadcast" (Machado, 2018, 14). Additional criticisms toward Acácio's representation were discussed in the popular media toward the end of the broadcast, with commentators asking questions such as "Who was Acácio? What was his role in the narrative? Did he have any purpose? The telenovela is coming to an end and we will never know, which makes him one of the worst characters in *Segundo Sol*" (Não vão deixar, 2018 para 9).

Finally, even though the poignant dialogues about race can be seen as a way to help spur discussions about racism in Brazil, the way in which the two most prominent Black bodies in *Segundo Sol*, Roberval and Acácio, were represented is surely problematic. As Ito (2017) states, the hypersexualization of the male Black body—the idealization of a Big Black man who is good in bed, wild and virile—is one of the main stereotypes that accompany the ideal of Black masculinity in Brazil. This construct is further complicated by the fact that because Black bodies are not usually considered a standard of beauty, rationality, or of belonging to a family man, fitting into to those types of stereotypes is often what they are left with. Ito states that to be a Black man in Brazil is to live with a series of stereotypes, which involve gender, race, and social class (para 1).

WHAT'S IN A NAME PART 2: ROBERVAL

I would like to end this chapter by highlighting once again the importance of names, especially family names, and their implications for characters' humanity, validity, and respect. Like Zefa, the Afro-Brazilian characters Roberval and Acácio were not given last names, or "proper" names. This omission serves as a powerful contributing factor toward the objectification of Black bodies, rendering them a characteristic of less-than: human, worthy, and so forth. In fact, in one of the exchanges between Severo Athayde and Roberval, the Black man's lack of a family name was highlighted and used to humiliate, subjugate, and oppress him. It also served to spark conversations around this theme, as I will demonstrate below:

In the episode that aired on July 19, 2018, Roberval, now rich and powerful, goes to visit Severo in jail, where Severo ended up after Roberval's scheming, trickery, and dramatic confrontations that are customary in telenovelas. Although the situation implies that Roberval has accrued some degree of power associated with his access to wealth, Severo will remind him that due to his race and lack of family name (more specifically, he implies, a white family's name), he is just not powerful "enough." As Pereira (2018) states, the dialogue is used to highlight Severo's racism and disdain toward his Black son (para 1).

Importantly, Roberval visits his father only after Zefa has begged him to help Severo. Roberval pretends to pity him, but really visits the prison because he thinks he can humiliate Severo further, who quickly reminds him of his inferior place in society more generally speaking, even if temporarily, he is incarcerated. Roberval approaches Severo in a traditional televised representation of a visiting room in a jail: it is a gray room with an old table, a lamp dangling overhead, gray walls and so forth. The scene is dark. Roberval stands tall in his suit while Severo is hunched at the other side of the table, his extremely red eyes signifying tiredness and lack of sleep. At first glance, Severo looks frail and distraught. But although Severo is in a terrible situation, he still acts as if he is in control. He asks Roberval if he came to savor his victory with his own eyes. As Roberval starts to answer that he "only came here to," he is abruptly interrupted by Severo, who tells his to "hit the road."

Roberval looks startled by Severo's attitude given the fact that he has lost his fortune and is in jail for fraud and money laundering. But before Roberval can say anything in response, Severo informs him that "there will not be any victory" for him, adding that no matter "where he is or how much money" he has, he will "always be Severo Athayde, a descendant of the Spaniards, a family that arrived there in the 1500s" and that his "family has ruled the state of Bahia ever since Bahia has existed." The dialogue reminds viewers of Brazil's history of both white colonization and slavery, in addition to lingering power imbalances of race, race relations and racism, in addition to the power associated with a family name (*Segundo Sol*, July 19, 2018).

As the scene progresses, Roberval, who has remained standing up to this point, responds by ridiculing Severo by saying that he has "so much power [yet] he finds himself in jail" and mockingly calls him "colonizer." Roberval tells Severo to look where he is at the moment and where Roberval is, as he pulls up a chair and now sits in front of his father. Severo sternly replies: "look, *boy*, you can put on all the fancy clothes you want, buy the most expensive car out there, you can live at a palace with one hundred workers"— here he pauses for a moment, leans on the desk, and defiantly moves his face closer to Roberval's—he "will always be a "bastard N*" (uses the N word equivalent). Roberval replies matter-of-factly: "Look at the way you speak," to which Severo doubles down: "nothing but a bastard." Pereira (2018) accurately describes this dialogue as "wide open racism" (para 6).

It is at this point in the confrontation that Roberval tells Severo that he is "only there because of my mother Zefa, not because of you, despicable human being." Severo replies that Roberval never cared about his mother as evidenced by his disappearance for twenty years and adds that the only thing he ever gave Zefa was heartache. When Roberval tells Severo he is paying for his lawyer, per Zefa's request, Severo mocks him once again, reminding Roberval that like in the past, Zefa has chosen to stay by his side and not her son's, adding that it must be a bitter pill to swallow. Severo states that Zefa's allegiance to him instead of Roberval is understandable, as no one in that house had ever liked him, and many always hoped that he would disappear (*Segundo Sol*, July 19, 2018).

At this moment it is Roberval who moves even closer toward Severo's face, and points his finger at him, shouting that this is not true. He reminds Severo that if he wants to see the light of day, he will have to deal with "This big N*" (uses the N word). Roberval concludes by pointing out that while Severo so proudly defends his family's name and honor, no one from the *Casa-Grande* (the traditional plantation family home) has come to his rescue. Here the audience can decode the dialogue as a reference to the seminal Brazilian book *Casa-Grande e Senzala/* "Masters and the Slaves," published in 1933 by Gilberto Freyre, about the formation of Brazilian society. The term *Casa-Grande/* "Big House" refers to the slave owner's master residence, usually on a sugarcane plantation, where whole towns were owned and managed by one man. *Senzala*, refers to the slave quarters. The promiscegenation book both underscores and reflects the racism and legacies of slavery that have long shaped Brazil. Freyre's work has been criticized for aiding the Racial Democracy ideology, which is being questioned in the dialogue between Severo Athayde and Roberval and can be questioned by viewers at home.

CONCLUSION

This chapter has provided an analysis of the Black characters Roberval and Acácio, two of the five main recurring Black characters in *Segundo Sol*, as well as compared their portrayals with that of the character Evilásio on the telenovela *Duas Caras*, which aired ten years prior. Through this comparative analysis, it has offered a glimpse into the ways in which Black males are represented in Brazilian telenovelas. The analysis revealed that the heterosexual male Black body, as seen through the lenses of primetime TV Globo telenovelas, presents audiences with a text filled with lingering stereotypes that encode such bodies in visual culture in the United States and Brazil, especially in the form of the hypersexualized Buck. However, a close reading of the telenovelas' texts reveals that the matter is not as, well . . . Black and white (pun intended). As revealed above, through provocative dialogue, the telenovela text can also serve to challenge longstanding racist discourses in Brazil, incite new ones, and raise questions about historical practices and the legacies of slavery in the country.

While negative Black male stereotypes were present and prominent in *Segundo Sol*, the audience was "active" in decoding such texts in an oppositional way, making their concerns heard and prompting changes in the narrative. This activism marked, as Fabrício Boliveira noted, a "true sign of the times" (Barros 2018a, para 2). Thus, the clash between the representation of Blacks and their social reality, the actions, and reactions to it, are a great example of how telenovelas, as problematic as they may be, can still act as agents of positive social change. Indeed, they have been and remain an important tool for understanding, constructing, and contesting social and race relations wherever they are broadcast.

It is important to underscore, however, that contesting representational stereotypes is not an automatic response among audiences: it requires engagement with the text and work on the part of the viewer. Voicing concerns—whether in public discussions, family settings, or through social media "activism"—it requires active labor associated with resisting such problematic systematic representational stereotypes, and their consequences to society as a whole. As Stuart Hall (1995) reminds us, stereotypes are key to the exercise of symbolic violence. They can be used in a shallow and superficial way to demonstrate patterns seen by the average society. As we have seen in the analysis offered in this chapter, stereotypes can also be used to reiterate conditions such as villainy, subordination, and sexualization, each of which has been long associated with heterosexual Black men in TV Globo's primetime telenovelas.

The most blatant identifiable stereotypes present in this investigation of Black men in primetime telenovelas were Black men as Bucks, Black men as Villains, and Black men as N*gg@s. As bell hooks (1992) notes, when encoded as hypersexual Bucks, this analysis demonstrates how, as bell hooks (1992) states, non-white bodies in popular culture are often seen as being sexual, worldly, and sensual. This was the case with Evilásio in *Duas Caras*, the first Black hero in a telenovela, and was also the case for Roberval and Acácio in *Segundo Sol*. For example, Roberval had sexual relationships with several women of various ages throughout the narrative, including his sister-in-law. He even worked as a prostitute for a while. Acácio was hypersexualized at the beginning *of Segundo Sol* yet was slowly written off of the telenovela and made irrelevant to the central plotlines. This unfortunately appears to support the notion that desires for—or fantasies about—the "Other" are exploited by consumer society in a way that preserves, rather than challenges, the status quo, since after being commodified and consumed the Other is (literally) forgotten. (hooks, 1992, p. 21).

While both Roberval and Acácio were clearly encoded as hypersexual, a characteristic unique to Roberval was his villainy, another lingering historical stereotype associated with Blacks in telenovelas. The crimes of which Black characters are portrayed as engaging in have ranged from petty theft to murder, to drug dealing, to arms trafficking. Yet Roberval's character was complex, and the provocative dialogues attributed to him led some in the press to identify him as *Segundo Sol*'s Black protagonist (Benício, 2018, para 4–6). But Roberval was no ordinary villain. The duality that was encoded to this character—he did criminal acts, but was also a victim of a racist family which lead to trauma—imposed in him and in the audiences a sort of Machiavellian question of does the end—revealing and punishing racism—justify the means? After all, he did plot several schemes which led his father to ruin, bankruptcy, and jail. And he humiliated every single Athayde family member, including his mother, by turning them into his personal service employees such as housekeeper, and cook. At the end *of Segundo* Sol, as is the norm in telenovelas, we see the resolution that is mostly associated with male white villains: redemption instead of death or jail (the usual ending for white female villains).[4]

Thus, Roberval's character seems to diverge from some of the historical portrayals encoded to Black bodies: According to Fabrício Boliveira, one of the most problematic aspects of representations of Black characters in telenovelas is that in that in most narratives, they still lack subjectivity, a problem associated with lack of diversity and inclusion on all levels of production (Potascheff, 2019, para 1). This was certainly not the case in Roberval's portrayal, even though the overall lack of diversity on all levels of production, as TV Globo admitted (as described in the introduction and chapter 1).

But while we can identify a type of subjectivity that was allowed to Roberval's character, we can also readily point to a lack of subjecthood. Most notably, like Zefa, Roberval and Acácio are not given a family name. This omission was highlighted in the dialogue of the show itself, in the confrontation between Severo Athayde and Roberval where the white patriarch tells Roberval his lack of a family name makes him nothing but a N*gg@ (with an "er" sound, not an "a" sound, at the end). Ironically, as noted by Benício (2018), while Roberval and Zefa did not have a last name referenced in the narrative, in real life, the full name of the actor who plays Roberval, "Fabrício Boliveira," appears all by itself in the opening credits. This had never happened before, even though Boliveira had acted in many other television and film productions. Since having an actors name stand along in the opening credits is usually reserved for leading actors, it is therefore a step forward for Blacks in Brazilian television (Benício, 2018, pp. 11–12).

Finally, as Hall (2006) reminds us, our identity is formed over time by unconscious processes: it is not something innate that exists at the moment of one's birth. In this sense, there is always a certain degree of something imagined about our identity; it is always in process, always being imagined, formed, created. As Hall suggests, the idea of identity as something finished should be replaced by "identification," which better captures the notion of something in progress (p. 39). What type of racial identity can be created and recreated through the representations of Blacks in telenovelas? The analysis in this chapter began to grapple with this and similar questions, which will continue to be pursued in the following chapters.

NOTES

1. This touches on the discussion in the previous chapter about "affective capital," by Hordge-Freeman (2015).

2. The game of capoeira is played in a circle, or *roda*.

3. Tupã is the name of the Guarani God, or creator.

4. For more on the representation of female villains in Brazilian telenovelas, see Joyce, S. N. & LaPastina, A. (2017). Women and criminality in Brazilian telenovelas: Salve Jorge and human trafficking (pp. 219–235). In Milly Buonanno (Ed). *Television Antiheroines. Women Behaving Badly in Crime and Television Dramas*. Intellect. Bristol: UK.

Chapter Four

Blackness beyond Black Bodies

Candomblé and Capoeira

In this chapter I examine the representation of two staples of Afro-Brazilian culture, heritage, and syncretism: Candomblé and Capoeira. Candomblé is the Afro-Brazilian religion that combines elements of Yoruba, Bantu and Catholicism, and was developed in Bahia by enslaved Africans. In *Segundo Sol,* Pai Didico ("Father Didico") is looking for a successor to lead his Candomblé *terreiro* (temple). A similar story line was present in *Duas Caras* with Mãe Setembrina ("Mother Setembrina"[1]) passing away and appointing Andréia Biju as the new leader of her religious community. While the recurrence of a story line about the underrepresented Afro-Brazilian religion may seem progressive, this chapter shows that the representation was at times problematic as it associated Candomblé with evil deeds, such as the killing of a white character. I will also briefly examine Capoeira, the Afro-Brazilian martial art that combines elements of fighting, acrobatics, music and dance, and which developed as a form of resistance to slavery in Brazil. In *Segundo Sol*, Capoeira was frequently shown in transition scenes and, as discussed in the previous chapter, provided opportunities to dissect and focus on the Black male body, both close up and in slow motion. My examination of Capoeira in *Segundo Sol* shows how it serves not merely as a way to perpetuate the hypersexual and virile Black body stereotype, but also highlights how it functions as a marker of lower social class. Indeed, the capoeiristas (those who practice the art) in *Segundo Sol* are all lower class and are Black or of mixed-race, even though the art today is practiced all over the world by individuals of all races and social classes. Finally, the representation of Capoeira in *Segundo Sol* suggests an othering of the art, making it strange and deviant in a hierarchical politicized way.

It is important to point out that these two expressions of Blackness—Candomblé and Capoeira—were present mainly during the beginning episodes of the telenovela, and slowly faded away as actual recurring story lines came to be increasingly merely used as visual transitions between scenes, places, characters and events, to eventually disappearing for months, only to come back during the final weeks of the broadcast. Importantly, it should be noted that Candomblé and Capoeira were not the only indirect references to Blackness in *Segundo Sol*: for example, there are numerous references to Carnaval and to the fact that the leading white character, Beto Falcão, was an Axé music singer.[2] The unique and vibrant colonial architecture of Bahia is often seen in aerial shots along with its beaches and churches as well as in other production elements such as diegetic and nondiegetic music: traditional samba, Axé, and Capoeira music.

As Soares (2012) states, historically Blackness in Brazil has been represented in the following ways: Blacks contributed to the country's foundation (a la Freyre); or Blacks have rhythm, sexual vigor, and tend to be immoral. These portrayals contrast sharply with the narrative of Brazil as a racial democracy. Indeed, discussions about race and racism are still taboo in the country, despite serious efforts by the Black and Feminist movements. Soares adds that Black activists often adopt traditional cultural practices such as samba and Capoeira in their attempts to highlight the dignity of their cultures and to build support around collective mobilization. However, Soares also notes that this celebration of Black heritage is frequently used as an ally to the plausibility of the racial democracy myth (pp. 76–77). In this sense, it seems fitting that TV Globo would incorporate such expressions of Blackness into the plot of *Segundo Sol*.

REPRESENTING CANDOMBLÉ

According to Port (2006), in the state of Bahia, the term Candomblé refers to various religious traditions of African origin that are centered around worshipping spiritual entities called *Orixás*. Each of these traditions seeks to establish reciprocal relationships between these spiritual beings and their human mediums through practices such as initiation, animal sacrifice, and possession. As the Port notes, practitioners of Candomblé have long been persecuted and marginalized in Brazil, yet over time Candomblé has become a symbol of the state of Bahia; along with capoeira, and aestheticized iconic images of Candomblé priestesses in elaborate lace dresses, baroque turbans, and colorful jewelry have served as key tools in the reimagination of the Brazilian nation as the unique mix of the white, Indian and Black races (pp. 446–447).

Since Candomblé is often used as a tool to perpetuate the myth of racial democracy in Brazil, it is no surprise that the first time it is referenced in *Segundo Sol* is in the beginning weeks of the narrative, being introduced by the white leading character Luzia/Ariella. In this scene, she is reunited with her daughter Manuela (Manu), even though Manu does not know that Luzia is in fact her mother who she has not seen for 18 years, since she was a small child. The two women are bonding while strolling around the streets of Salvador, the capital of Bahia, with its brightly colored architecture on full display. Ariella then enters a store and buys a gift for her daughter, a *patuá*: a uniquely Brazilian protection necklace with several charms associated with Candomblé. Ariella tells Manuela that "this will protect you from all evil" (*Segundo Sol*, May 26, 2018). Brazilian researcher and historian Vanicléia Santos explains that the word "Patuá" has its origin in the Brazilian Indian language Tupi, with the word meaning basket, or chest, in which protective ingredients were placed. Since the eighteenth century, however, it has also been used to refer to amulets worn by Africans and their descendants in Brazil (Vanicléia Santos: O patuá, para 2). For this reason, Santos notes that there is a debate among linguists about whether this word should be considered a Tupinism or Africanism within the context of Brazilain Portuguese.

As the scene goes on, Ariella and Manu also buy a traditional Bahian dish—a Vatapá—from a smiling street vendor dressed in traditional white laced Candomblé clothes and adorned with beads. Moments later after this manufactured aesthetic representation of Brazil's diversity and so-called racial utopia, Manu leaves her mother and meets her then boyfriend Acácio at his Capoeira practice. Once again, Acácio is represented as a hypersexual Black body: he is shirtless and barefoot, which is not uncommon for a Capoeira *roda*. However, as Acácio and Manu leave to go to Acácio's home, the occupied house where he has started his community (the *Casarão*), we see Acácio walking the streets while remaining shirtless and barefoot, giving him a somewhat "primitive" character (*Segundo Sol*, May 26, 2018).

The second time in the series that Candomblé is portrayed is from the episode that aired on June 9, when Doralice, a recurring Black character, married to the leading white male's brother (Ionã), visits her father's "temple" (*terreiro*). According to Port (2006), the purpose of the *terreiro* is, among other things, to "oversee the initiation of spirit mediums and to organize the yearly cycle of rituals and festivities honoring the *Orixás.*" Additionally, *terreiros* operate as "markets for salvation commodities" (*mercados dos bens de salvação*), as they aim to generate income by providing spiritual, divinatory, and curative services to its customers comprised of "cultists" and "non-cultists" alike (p. 446). In this scene with Doralice, we see her in the *terreiro*, which appears to be a forested backyard decorated with flowers and plants. We can also see in the background women happily working—cooking, cleaning, and performing other domestic tasks—in their white lace dresses and hair turbans. The atmosphere is overall pleasant and calm.

As Doralice sees her father, Pai Didico, she kisses his hand and asks for his blessing, to which he replies "May *Oxalá* bless you."[3] He then tells her that she cannot go for so long without coming to the house/temple. He is wearing the traditional white attire associated with Candomblé, along with beaded necklaces also associated with different *Orixás* (deities). Pai Didico offers her a meal as he tells her that she "was born on Saint Barbara's day, Iansã" and that "Iansã is the Female spirit of winds and storms who is impulsive and a warrior, as well as very passionate," which seems to accurately capture Doralice's character as seen thus far in the telenovela: Doralice is often seen throwing fits of jealousy and rage toward her husband.

As the scene progresses, Pai Didico tells Doralice she was the best gift her mother has ever given him, and that this house of worship is his legacy to her. He clarifies that he does not mean just the land and the physical house, but the spiritual heritage that it all represents. He adds that the place is a "lighthouse for various lost people." The scene is calm, set outside in a beautiful garden, and shot at night with low, warm light. This representation of Candomblé as conveying warmth and safety can be read as a positive portrayal of a minority religion, considering that Brazil is predominantly Catholic with a growing Evangelical population.

As their conversation proceeds, we see a striking similarity with a plot line in *Duas Caras*, ten years prior, as I will demonstrate: Pai Didico tells Doralice he is "not that old," but also "not that young," and that he is "tired." Doralice places her hand over his and replies that she understands the increasing challenges of age but adds that she wants to be a "common person, go to school, graduate college and become a nutritionist, take care of her home, husband, and kids." She finally adds that she therefore "can't" remain in the family home and operate the *terreiro*. To this her father replies that she was "born in that house and that her crib is Candomblé." He adds that he does not have time to teach anyone else the mysteries of the religion, and furthermore, that some things you do not teach, since they are inborn: he stresses to Doralice that she was born with this gift and mission. He goes on to say, "think about it, my queen. Just think about this, my daughter, this is all I ask." Doralice replies that she has thought about it over and over as he knows, and that he will have to find a replacement. He replies that she was always the boss of him, always doing what she wants, the perfect daughter of *Oyá*" (the Yoruba name for Yansã) (*Segundo Sol*, June 9, 2018)."

This resistance from an Afro-Brazilian woman, the "natural descendant" of the leader of the *terreiro* and a born leader in her own right, marks a rejection of her heritage, tradition, and family beliefs. The story line is extremely similar to one from *Duas Caras* ten years earlier. In *Duas Caras,* one plot focus on Mãe Setembrina, the leader of a Candomblé *terreiro,* who tells the character Andréia Biju that the *Orixás* have chosen her to be the next leader.

But Andréia does not want the job, as her dream is to be another type of leader: the "Drum Queen" (*Rainha de Bateria*) in a school of samba during the traditional Carnaval parade. The repetition of this story line could be seen as marking a lack of imagine among the writers, and their inability to tell multiple different stories involving Candomblé. Further, it can be read as problematic since each plotline involves a young Black woman choosing to abandon her African spiritual roots. On the other hand, these plots can be read as positive simply for the fact that they feature Candomblé prominently in a primetime television program. As Joyce (2012) demonstrates, during the airing of *Duas Caras*, journalists praised the story line as a disruptive moment in a traditionally racist society, particularly one that had a long history of denigrating Afro-Brazilian cultures and religion (p. 75).

While in *Segundo Sol* Doralice is the heir to the *terreiro*, which comes with a leadership position, her most notable personal characteristic is her extreme insecurity; for example, she is a jealous wife even though she has a loving and faithful husband, Ionã. At one point, she is so blinded by her emotions and passion (this goes back to her father's description of her as the daughter *Oyá*) that she hires a woman to seduce her husband in order to prove to that he is indeed a cheater (her plan does not work). Doralice also slaps and hits him, leaving him bruised, for example in the episode that aired on May 5. In this sense, she fits a stereotype common in American television culture: that of the angry Black woman.

This stereotype is also on display in the episode that aired on June 26, when Doralice visits her father again at the *terreiro*. She does so after having discovered that Ionã's partner at work (he is a police officer) is a woman. In Doralice's view, this situation represents a marital betrayal. She asks Pai Didico to ask the *Orixás* if Ionã is cheating on her. The audience then sees Pai Didico perform a *Jogo de Búzios* (literally translated into "cowry shell game"). According to Voeks (1997), The *búzios* constitutes the principal means of exchange and communication between humans and the pantheon of African deities. Voeks adds that the *Orixá Exu* is the deity that is most integral to the success of the *búzios*. As the owner of streets and crossroads, the arteries of communication, Exu symbolically directs traffic between the parallel worlds of Aiyê (the realm of the mortals) and Orum (the realm of spirits). During divination, via the *jogo de búzios*, Exu transmits messages from the divinities to the *terreiro* priest or priestess, who in turn translates their meanings for other human beings (p. 45).

After interpreting the *búzios*, Pai Didico reveals to Doralice that he sees a woman in Ionã's future. Doralice proceeds to tell her father that she is going to give her husband a "pre-beating"—she will beat him up even before anything happens—just to teach him a lesson. This is not only problematic due to the racist characteristic of the "angry Black woman" trope, but also because it exemplifies another problematic yet common trope of Brazilian telenovelas, as discussed by Joyce and Martinez (2017): that of intimate partner domestic violence, where abuse is portrayed as comical and justifiable when the woman is the perpetrator. As the scene progresses, Pai Didico tries to calm Doralice down, reminding her that just because he sees a woman in Ionã's future, it does not mean he will have a relationship with her. Additionally, he tells her again that she should follow his footsteps by inheriting the *terreiro*. But once again, Doralice says she will not, because she has other dreams for her life, such as to get a bachelor's degree in Nutrition. Pai Didico finally says that he thinks she will be able to help more people as the leader of the *terreiro* but that ultimately, he cannot force her to take a path she does not desire to take, and that it is ultimately her choice. Doralice concludes the conversation by telling her father not to keep his hope up.

A few weeks after Doralice refuses to assume the role of leader of the *terreiro*, Pai Didico is shown looking for a replacement. What comes as a surprise is that the role goes to one of Pai Didico's "adopted sons," Groa, who is the best friend of a leading white character and portrayed as her "savior" when she is in trouble. Namely, Groa is the one who helps the "heroine" escape from Brazil to Iceland (where he is originally from) and is responsible for turning her into an internationally successful DJ. He is also the one who later brings her back to Brazil under a new name and appearance. Throughout the show, Groa is her loyal confidant. Interestingly, Groa will be the next leader of the *terreiro*, home to an Afro-Brazilian religion, yet is white-skinned, blond-haired, and has green eyes: he is a *gringo* from Iceland. His ascendancy to a leadership position can therefore be read as part of a "white savior trope," which serves to help advance the racial democracy myth as previously described by Port (2006). Indeed, the racial democracy myth enables one to read Candomblé not only as an Afro Brazilian religion, but as a religion for all.

Groa's backstory is worth examining in closer detail. According to Vieira (2018b), Groa is the son of an Icelandic woman with a Brazilian *Pai de Santo* ("Father of Saints," akin to a High Priest), whom he has never met. In search of his father, Groa ends up at Pai Didico's *terreiro*. As soon as he steps in the house, he is spiritually moved and falls in love with Candomblé. Even though he is not Pai Didico's real son, the *Pai de Santo* figuratively adopts him as such. The *terreiro* is also where he meets Luzia, the main heroine (para 1–5), creating yet another link between the white and Black worlds of Bahia, supposedly a microcosm of Brazil's racial utopia. After Doralice refuses to assume leadership of the terreiro, Pai Didico will slowly groom Groa to take the role.

One scene is particularly revealing in terms of Groa's devotion to Candomblé and Pai Didico comes from the episode that aired on June 19.

In it, Groa is having lunch with Pai Didico in the *terreiro*. The establishing shots show the *terreiro* being cleaned by women in their white lace dresses and head scarves. They are also cooking to the sound of African drums. The atmosphere is once again pleasant and welcoming, which can be read as a positive representation of the traditionally underrepresented and negatively stereotyped religion. As they start their meal, Pai Didico uses a saltshaker, and Groa asks: "Oh, father, are you really going to eat all that salt?" Pai Didico replies: "Oh my son, I like to taste the salt and I am way too old not to have these simple pleasures in life." The audience knows that the reference to salt has to do with Pai Didico's poor health and is used as a foreshadowing device to signal his impending death. Groa then teases him saying, "well let's hope your doctor will not hear about this," to which Didico replies that "he will only hear about it if you tell him." Both men laugh (*Segundo Sol*, June, 19, 2018).

As the scene continues, Pai Didico tells Groa that he is "very special," and thanks him for all the love and care he has shown him and the *terreiro* over the years. Groa says he is the one who is thankful for being sheltered and welcomed there, and that Pai Didico is like a real father to him: "The loving Dad I never had." Pai Didico says that it makes him very happy to hear those words, and reminds Groa that he has a beautiful spiritual journey ahead of him; he insists that Groa come to the *terreiro* more often, as he needs him there. Groa replies that he is a mere outsider to the *terreiro*, a *gringo* as he is often called, and a mere spectator and researcher of Candomblé. But Pai Didico insists that Groa did not end up at the *terreiro* by random chance, that he was in fact listening to the calling of the *Orixás* and that he has a priestly mission in the house. Pai Didico adds that he may need Groa sooner than he had imagined, as he is tired and old, and, furthermore, his daughter Doralice wants nothing to do with the *terreiro*, which brings us back to Groa's remarks about the sault and his worries about his health *(Segundo Sol*, June 19, 2018).

Pai Didico then finally comes out and directly tells Groa that he will be his successor. Groa says that this is an absurd idea, and that he is not worthy or deserving of the honor. Pai Didico assures him that he is indeed ready and must keep the good works of the *terreiro* going, and that he completely trusts Groa as one of his oldest and dearest "sons."[4] He concludes that he has fulfilled all of his *obligations* to becoming an amazing Babalorixá—the Yoruba word that means a High Priest in Candomblé and Umbanda. According to Port (2006), in Candomblé, as an initiation cult, knowledge of the secrets and mysteries of the religion can only be obtained through lengthy periods of initiation and that knowledge comes with doing: observing the taboos, participating in the rituals, subjecting oneself to the rigid temple hierarchy, and respecting one's commitment to the *Orixás*. Thus, time is crucial to the transmission of knowledge: year after year cultists go through the motions of the rituals and ceremonies, and with the passing of time the knowledge that Candomblé seeks to instill is gained by a new generation of leaders and adherents (p. 448).

As the scene continues, Groa speaks in a loud shaky voice that he is *Ebômi*, meaning someone with experience and privileges, but not the highest "Father"/ "Priest." While he enjoys helping people, he does not think himself capable of reading the búzios, and is afraid of the responsibilities that his proposed new position would entail. But Pai Didico tells Groa that has the strength of a Babalorixá and will become a Saint right then and there: "Trust me, do not resist, become an instrument." As Pai Didico speak this, we see a ritual taking place through dance and music. Groa looks like he in a trance but comes out of it and says he simply cannot keep going, that it is too much energy for him to handle. He asks for forgiveness and leaves (*Segundo Sol*, June 19, 2018). Several episodes later, Groa goes back to the *terreiro*. Here we see Pai Didico asking Groa to ask the *Orixás* weather he should take over the house; Pai Didico also throws the Búzios. When the *Orixá*s confirm that Groa, a white foreigner, will be the leader of the *terreiro*, Pai Didico says that his daughter will take a different path, even though she is his biological daughter, because he does not decide the future, the *Orixás* do, and that Groa, willvbecome the successor and heir of the "house" (*Segundo Sol*, June 29, 2018).

While it may seem that Candomblé held a place of prominence in the story line of *Segundo Sol*, its significance within the overall narrative actually decreased as the program developed, only to reemerge again near the end of the telenovela. This was noted in the popular press, including by Machado (2018) who stated that "João Acaiabe's (Pai Didico) character seemed to have a promising plot at first" (para 4), and that "the story could have addressed a number of issues such as religion and intergenerational conflict." However, as Machado noted, "Pai Didico only made sporadic appearances during the telenovela, giving at most some advice to Luzia (Giovanna Antonelli) here and there." Similarly, Farias (2018a) also pointed out that Pai Didico, who seemed to have a promising and strong presence in the plot, practically disappeared (para 1) from the narrative as the program went on. The storylines involving Pai Didico were so sporadic that it prompted backlash in the popular press with some noting that he had only appeared six times and that at the time they were writing the article, Didico had disappeared from the plot and the screen for an entire month, adding that the actor himself (João Acaiabe) was disappointed as he had expected the character to be much bigger (Farias 2018a, para 2–4).

The abrupt ending to both the Candomblé narrative and the story line of Pai Didico was also felt by the actor who played him: João Acaiabe described always being on "stand by," and stated that if he would have taken other job opportunities during the show if offered them. Acaiabe added that he had always thought that Pai Didico would be a much bigger character and that he was just left waiting and wondering for weeks on end whether he would work or not. This is important as we know that the production of telenovelas happen on a daily basis. After months of not appearing on screen, Acaiabe finally came back for one scene near the end to fulfill his mission: to die and to pass the *terreiro* to Groa (Machado, 2018, para 5–6). Yet despite being frustrated with the lack of weight given to the character, Acaiabe nonetheless praised his story line, stating that "the very presence of the character is extremely important, mainly because it happens in Bahia, but also because it is something from Brazil." Acaiabe added that "Pai de Santo and Babalorixá are psychologists for those who have no money," and that this is a "very strong heritage."

In his comments about his role on *Segundo Sol*, João Acaiabe also spoke about how his character resonated on a deeply personal level:

> During slavery, God was taken from away from those who came from Africa. I myself, as a Black man, did not have this information. I was raised in the Catholic Church. It was on TV Tupi, when I also played a *Pai de Santo* character [in "The Prophet"/ O Profeta, in 1977], that I discovered this universe. Now at 74 years old, I have become more attentive to the Candomblé religion and I see a *Pai de Santo* in São Paulo. I try to learn more and more. He gave me some cowrie shells so I could practice with him, but in the *telenovela* I use scenographic ones (Farias 2018a, paras 7–9).

The actor's introspection about his own lack of understanding of Afro religions until he was confronted with playing a practitioner of the faith highlights the historical attempt by the Catholic Church to convert native Indians and Blacks in Brazil, but also the lingering stereotype of using onscreen Black characters in a segregated "Black universe," which can include ghettos and casting them as villains or as candomblé priests/priestesses.

Telenovelas are a complex site of mediations, that we know. So, while some representations of Black characters rely on and reinforce longstanding stereotypes, it can still be noteworthy that a Black religion is portrayed in a primetime telenovela. As Acaiabe points out, "This discussion is important because if you don't tolerate other religions, how are you going to get anywhere? There's an African phrase, in ubuntu, that says: 'I am because you are, because we are.' You have to respect other religions to get somewhere." The actor added that although he was a practicing Catholic, he had been studying the Candomblé religion, in order to play the character with "great dignity, as he represents his ancestors," and reminded viewers that for a "long time the practice of worshiping *Orixás* was hidden, and even persecuted by the police, and that now persecutions happen in another ways" (Farias 2018b, para 3).

In a joint interview given by Acaiabe and Roberta Rodrigues (the actress who plays his daughter Doralice), Rodrigues also addressed the cultural, religious, and social persecution suffered those who practice Candomblé. Her calling attention to this reality once again highlights the inaccuracy of the myth of racial democracy: "Candomblé is so marginalized that those who practice it are ashamed to say it." The actress adds that if there is one thing Brazilians do well, and better than anyone else in the world, it is creating telenovelas, and that in Brazil they are a type of religion in the sense that the things represented in them become "truth." Thus, how you represent Afro-Brazilianess is an important issue. As Acaiabe, observes "People have a prejudice against these religions]" and highlights that much of "telenovelas' influence comes from the fact that they invade people's homes at dinner time. Anything you talk about, discuss, can lead to something, in real life and should never be taboo. My hope is that people understand it can respect it. You may not agree with another religion, but you respect each other's freedom," he said (Farias 2018b, para 4–9).

While story lines involving Candomblé were generally portrayed in what can be read as in a positive light, for example in matters of inclusion, the mere fact that it was represented as a legitimate religion, but also due to the dialogues between Pai Didico, Doralice, and Groa, where the practice is associated with helping people and performing good deeds. However, after Pai Didico dies, Afro-Brazilian religions come back into the narrative of *Segundo Sol*, but not in a good way: the positive representation of both Afro Brazilian religions and Pai Didico were short lived (pun intended). Specifically, after disappearing from the narrative for several weeks, Afro-Brazilian religions are portrayed again in a scene that mixes Candomblé, Umbanda, and Macumba without a clear distinction between them, and in a way that associates these Afro-Religions with evil deeds. According to Nascentes (2017), *Umbanda* is a Bantu term synonymous with *Macumba*, an Afro-Brazilian religion constituted in Brazil and stemming from influences of Spiritism (*Espiritismo*), Bantu and Candomblé. While *Macumba* no longer invokes the spirit of Bantu ancestors in Africa as it once did, it now invokes the spirit of Brazilian ancestors, both Black and Indian. *Macumba* evolved into *Umbanda*, which honors *Caboclos* (a Brazilian of mixed white and indigenous or Black and indigenous ancestry) (p. 89).

In the *Segundo Sol* episode that aired on September 10, the character Laureta (the lead white villain) orders the killing of another white character, her brother. She is shown in a ritualistic scene giving offerings and praying to *Orixás* to help her on her mission in a comical, disrespectful and misleading way. Once again, as illustrated in chapter 1 (From Active to Active-ism), audiences flooded social media to express concern, disapproval, and disgust over the portrayal. For example, one twitter user stated: "Thank you, thank you, João Emanuel Carneiro (The author of the telenovela) for supporting the religious intolerance of African religions with this scene of Laureta praising *Exu* after ordering murder!" Another Twitter user declared that "Laureta making an offering to the *Orixás* after ordering Remy to be murdered reinforces the myth that Candomblé is used to do evil to others." Such comments were not unique to Twitter. A Facebook page dedicated to the religion, called *Aldeia Caboclo Flecheiro*, posted an article clarifying the true meaning of *Exu* and *Pomba Gira* (the Orixás named by Laureta in the scene), and expressed disapproval of their portrayal in the telenovela: "The character makes a plan to murder someone and then makes an offering to *Pomba Gira* and asks for help from the *Orixás* and *Exu*. In prime time. Thank you, Rede Globo for sending everything we fought against down the drain! Exu does not do evil, *Pomba Gira* does not do evil" (*Segundo Sol* polemiza, September 11, 2018).

The popular press also devoted significant attention to the controversial episode, highlighting that Afro-Brazilian religious leaders were offended with the overall scene and its accompanying dialogue, particularly the part in which Laureta states "I want all the celestial beings, spirits and *Exus*, united. I need everything to help me right now," in reference to the murder-for-hire scheme she had just set in motion. According to Carneiro (2008), Exu is an ambassador/messenger for the mortals to the *Orixá Xangô* (p. 70). In one news story about this scene, the reporter highlighted the immediate and passionate response that appeared on the web after the scene aired, with activists calling out the writer of the telenovela with twitter posts such as: "How ridiculous to demonize the figure of Exu in the telenovela. Exu is not a demon and does no harm to anyone." Another Twitter user asked the question: "Where are the federations and the religious leaders? Exu is life, path, strength, light. Exu is an *Orixá* and messenger of the energy of God." And another tweet cited by the story reads:

> After so much struggle to undo the prejudice existing in Afro religions, to show that *Exu* and *Pomba Gira* are not part of evil, to understand that those who do evil are not *Orixás* . . . and there goes the telenovela reinforcing ignorance and prejudice. . . . The large audience that watches the telenovela has a version presented to them and has no idea what *Exu* and *Pomba Gira* mean. This scene only reinforces prejudice and associates evil with such religions (Cena de 'Segundo Sol' gera polêmica, September 11, 2008, paras 1–3)

On another social media platform, Instagram, the Umbanda Priest Alexandre Cumino shared a photo of the scene with the following caption: "*Exu* is not a Devil!" He added that "Yesterday, while we were at *Pena*

Branca School extolling, loving and reverencing *Exu* and *Pomba Gira*—the broadcaster (which has a public license), in its prime time and to in its largest audience—for the primetime telenovela '*Segundo Sol*' associated the image of *Exu* and *Pomba Gira* with human evil." The priest added that,

> This is sad for our *terreiro* culture, sad for Umbanda and Candomblé, sad for a Brazilian people who are unaware of their ancestral values and diverse origins that shape this syncretic Brazilian culture, but it is also sad to know that in fact many people light candles to their ignorance itself, believing that *Exu* responds to our ego, also known as "human evil." *Exu* the *Orixá* deity or *Exu* the *Umbanda* Entity does not "serve" human beings as "servants," or "servers" of our childish material condition, which is short-sighted, narrow-minded, mediocre and small. *Exu* and *Pomba Gi*ra are really BIG. *EXU* is irreverent and it is possible that He himself created the controversy to generate polemic, and who knows, to awaken in the respectable and notorious broadcaster the importance of researching and contextualizing better everything that involves faith and community (Cena de 'Segundo Sol' gera polêmica, 9/11/2008, para 4)

Taiane Macedo, the spiritual leader of the Umbanda Mystic Center Oxum Apará (Centro de Umbanda Mística Oxum Apará (CUMOA)) also joined in the widespread critique of the scene, explaining that "*Exu* is always controversial, irreverent, but lack of knowledge generates ignorance. Knowledge is not understanding. Everyone knows or has heard of the name *Exu*, but they do not know what or who he is." Macedo added that "in reality, to give erroneous credit to *Exu* is to cast our own shadow and human evil on him. This is regrettable for the religions that fight against discrimination and that worship that entity. Our Umbanda understands this *Orixá* and this and entity as a great guardian, who protect and guide us." Macedo concluded that we must "know and study" Afro-Brazilian religions because "ignorance leads to this" (Cena de 'Segundo Sol' gera polêmica, September 11, 2008, para 5).

In response to the controversy surrounding the scene with Laureta making ritualistic offerings and praying to *Orixás*, TV Globo issued a statement claiming that the scene was not a reference to any one religion: as the network insisted, "Laureta asks for protection from the stars, spirits, *Orixás*. . . . From the world beyond, without referring to any religion specifically." TV Globo added that "we should also point out that, as it is registered at the end of each episode,[5] telenovelas are works of fiction, and it is also worth mentioning that Laureta is a villain, and therefore exhibits several objectionable attitudes that only make sense in the context of dramaturgy" (Guaraldo, 2018, para 11). Thus, with the excuse that telenovelas are works of fiction and that villains do awful things, TV Globo perpetuated racist stereotypes associated with Afro-Brazilian religions: that they do the work of the devil; that they are less than, foreign, "other." Similar representations were also used when Capoeira was portrayed.

REPRESENTING CAPOEIRA

While a more detailed textual analysis of Capoeira was presented in chapter 3 (*His Body: Slaves, Bucks, Villains and N*gg@s*), due to the fact that the Black character Acácio was its main practitioner on *Segundo Sol*, it is worth taking a moment to reexamine Capoeira here, as a manifestation of Blackness in Bahia and in Brazil. Broadly, Capoeira was used in transition scenes to add cultural flavor and to visually portray Blackness. In these transitions, scenes of Capoeira were usually paired with images of picturesque aerial shots of Salvador: the architecture, the ocean, and nature served to establish a visually appealing background, with the camera then slowly zooming in on the Capoeira *roda* and the players—usually Acácio and Manu's brother, Ícaro.

As Soares (2012) states, using famous Brazilian settings alongside representations of Capoeira is a device that works in global products such as telenovelas, as cities like Rio de Janeiro and Salvador are known internationally for their engagement with Black Brazilian culture such as samba, Afro-Brazilian food, and Capoeira. Indeed, much of the Brazilian tourism industry is organized around these products, alongside the country's luxurious beaches (p. 78). A Capoeira *roda* with the beach as backdrop was in fact the device used as a transition time lapse production tool in an interesting way where we see two kids playing Capoeira, one Black and one white, and after a few strategic cuts to close up to the instruments: the berimbau, the atabaque, hands clapping, the camera goes back to the players inside the *roda* to show them as young adults. The audience will eventually realize, through close-ups of the boy's faces, that they are in fact Acácio and Ícaro. A title on the screen lets the audience know that we are in Salvador, Bahia, and that the year is now 2018 (*Segundo Sol*, May 24, 2018).

Moments after this scene which uses Capoeira to transport the reader ahead in time by twenty years, we see Manu nearby watching her brother Ícaro and her boyfriend Acácio play Capoeira. This is the scene that sets up the birthday scene analyzed in chapter 3, when Acácio is mistaken by Manu's white family to be a waiter at the dinner party. It is also the first time we hear Acácio speak, although as audience members, we have already been introduced to every aspect of his strong, Black body. Manuela tells Acácio, referring to him in the third person, that "My boyfriend is the best *capoeirista* in all of Bahia. It looks like you can fly away from the *roda*" (*Segundo Sol*, May 24, 2018).

Other than the few times we see Acácio playing in a roda in scenes where he is being objectified, and therefore used against Blackness and its own inheritance of resistance to oppression and affirmation, Capoeira was used merely as scenery, background, and as transition devices between scenes. In such scenes, where Capoeira is used as a visual and aesthetic expression of culture, and serves as a unifying device: a beautiful and rich cultural manifestation of Blackness that is for the enjoyment of all Bahians, and all Brazilians. In this sense, Capoeira works to advance the myth of racial democracy.

Another way in which we can read the use of Capoeira *in Segundo Sol* is as a manifestation of class. Namely, in addition to being associated with Black people, Capoeira is also often used to show that characters are of a lower socioeconomic class. For example, when Capoeira is actually written into a scene, and not used merely as a visual device, it is only practiced by characters from the "poor" segment of (the telenovela) society. For example, when Rochelle seeks Acácio in a *Roda de Capoeira*, and insinuates herself to him, Acácio replies that he never thought a "classy and elegant girl like her would ever be interested in a guy like him—a Capoeira" (Segundo Sol, May 25, 2020). The dialogue can be read with ambiguity as well, since, as discussed, race and class are so intertwined in Brazil, the audience could read "a Capoeira" in this dialogue to mean "Black man," or "poor man," or both. Thus, like the Afro-Brazilian religions, particularly Candomble, Capoeira in *Segundo Sol* is set apart and depicted as an "other" (a la bell hooks): exotic, different, foreign.

CONCLUSION

As Esther Hamburger (1998) has argued, Brazilian telenovelas are the glue that holds Brazilian society together. The centrality of the genre helps underscore the importance of the foregoing study of the representation of Black characters in *Segundo Sol*, not just Black bodies, and the subsequent discussions revolving around what it means to be Black in contemporary Brazil. This involved examining cultural manifestations of Blackness, particularly Capoeira and Candomblé. As I demonstrated, these portrayals were not done in a way that celebrated Black culture and heritage; by studying them through critical lens, we can see that they actually helped perpetuate some negative stereotypes. Perhaps most significantly, as Soares (2012) reminds us, one of the perils of turning such manifestations into a type of a celebrated spectacle is that these representations can be used to advance to the racial democracy ideology, as they provide proof that there are no real racial divisions in Brazil (in contrast, for example, to those that exist in countries such as South Africa and the United States) and that all Brazilians are racially mixed, and almost all like to party at Carnaval (p. 76).

As discussed above, the story line about Candomblé in *Segundo Sol* was reminiscent and almost identical to one that took place ten year prior in *Duas Caras,* where an elderly leader of a *terreiro* look for his replacement. On one hand, this repetition may point to a narrow, one-dimensional type of representation of Candomblé. On the other hand, the fact that it is represented on primetime can be seen as a positive aspect of telenovelas and Brazilian cultural acceptance of Afro-Brazilian heritage. As Lopes (2004) reminds us, "stories narrated on television are, above all, important for their cultural significance, offering precious material to understand the culture and society of which they are an expression of" (p. 125).

While it is true that *Segundo Sol* at times framed Candomblé as a religion for all people, while still being rooted in Afro-Religion and heritage—for example, the fact that the lead white actress practices it, or at least "borrows" from it in a syncretic way as seen throughout the broadcast. Moreover, the fact that the show ends with a white foreigner (Groa) set to become the next high priest in Pai Didico's *terreiro*. However, at the same time, it is portrayed with disdain by one of the few Black women in the plot: namely, Doralice does not want to assume leadership of her father's *terreiro*. Likewise, in *Duas Caras*, Andréia Biju did not want to lead Mãe Setembrina's *terreiro* either. It is also worth remembering that after having disappeared from the narrative for weeks, Afro-Brazilian religions came back to *Segundo Sol* only to be associated with evil deeds.

The other manifestation of "Blackness beyond Black bodies" highlighted in this chapter was Capoeira, a staple of resistance and liberation by Afro-Brazilians. Unfortunately, what this examination revealed was that the Afro-Brazilian martial art was ultimately used as a means of helping to perpetuate lingering stereotypes about Blacks and Blackness: Capoeira was portrayed as a marker of lower class and as a means through which to direct viewer attention to the hypersexual and virile male heterosexual Black body. Acácio, for example, was usually shown shirtless and sweaty. Visually, the camera focused on parts of his body such as his abs, arms, lips, and muscular physique, as he performs kicks and flies through the air. Narratively, his hypersexuality was underscored by his having a threesome, various sexual partners, being compared to "delicious" food, and being othered (as conceptualized by bell hooks [1992]). He was an exotic delight to be savored, consumed and later forgotten: in *Segundo Sol*, he disappeared from the show almost entirely as the narrative progressed.

Coupled with the fact that both story lines about Blackness were mainly present in the beginning of the broadcast, this investigation shows that while there is room in primetime telenovelas for the inclusion of diverse racial story lines, longstanding anti-Black stereotypes unfortunately persist, which serve to deny or diminish the experiences, humanity, subjectivity, contributions, and worth of Black Brazilians.

NOTES

1. In Candomblé a "Mother of Saints" (*Mãe de Santo*) is a type of priestess running a *terreiro* and a "Father of Saints" (*Pai de Santo*) is the priest.

2. Axé music is a genre that originated in the city of Salvador in Bahia in the 1980s. It combines various Afro-Caribbean styles such as Reggae and Calypso with Brazilian Rythms from the Northeast such as *frevo* and *forró*. The white male lead was a staple of the Bahian Carnaval, and a successful Axé singer who had long (blond) dreadlocks in the beginning of the saga. Additionally, literally speaking, according to Port (2006), the word Axé means "the life-generating force that candomblé seeks to accumulate and transmit" (p. 453).

3. *Oxalá* is the eldest *Orixá*, regarded as the father of all *Orixás*.

4. Pai Didico is referring to his position as "Father of Saints."

5. It is customary to have this statement at the end credits of telenovelas.

Conclusion

The research presented in this book about the representation of Blacks and Blackness in Brazilian television, and more specifically in the country's TV Globo telenovelas, is a continuation of my previous investigation, in *Brazilian Telenovelas and the Myth of Racial Democracy*, (2012). Analyzing televised representations of social groups in Brazilian telenovelas is important not least because Brazilians still "watch TV,"[1] and telenovelas. Importantly, the comparison between *Segundo Sol* (2018) to *Duas Caras* (2008), which my two books affords, does not just continue the investigation of representations of Blacks in telenovelas: it is also part of a research continuum that understands the telenovela as a tool for racial and social transformation and justice, since the medium offers not only limitations as far as suggestions about "what is," but also empowers viewers to imagine "what could be." As we have seen, both telenovelas themselves and the online activism they have spurred can be key vehicles through which to construct a public sphere encompassing a plurality of voices and subjectivities.

My comparative analysis also went beyond looking only at expressions of Blackness in Brazilian productions by comparing such representations to (North) American productions, and drawing on research about the latter. As previously highlighted, the reliance on similar stereotypes across North (United States) and South media, two power players in the Global visual market (ex: Hollywood and TV Globo), serves to shed light on parallels in the racial landscape across cultures within the same hemisphere. Likewise, similarities in the racial discourses say something about debates and attitudes about race around the world, since American and Brazilian productions circulate globally. And, while my examination has shown a persistent pattern of stereotypes in the representation of Blacks in TV Globo primetime telenovelas, it has also shown how telenovelas ultimately function as a lively, fertile ground for changes in hegemonic discourses, as well as a vector to challenge manufactured ideas about race and what it means to be Black. In our current state of high connectivity and convergence culture, resistance manifests itself online, then onscreen, in fantasy and reality, in a never-ending cycle—where decoders become encoders, where the audience goes from passive receivers to active audiences to activists.

The Brazilian case is complicated and highly interesting: while racism is persistent in various segments of society, and the idea of the country being a utopian racial paradise is challenged from time to time, the racial democracy myth still persists in various manifestations, not only in telenovelas. For example, it was foregrounded in the Brazilian bid for the 2016 Olympics, when Brazil "engaged in a politics of self-exotification by extending its image of a peaceful sensual racial democracy" to the world at large (Mitchell, 2020, p. 205).

Thus, while most Brazilians like to imagine and sell their country as a type of racial utopia—or democracy—due to years of miscegenation creating a mixed-race and multicultural population, the reality is that, as in the United States, Brazil is rife with racism and white supremacy. This is partly reflected in racist media portrayals, a lingering and (trans)national problem across the United States and Brazil which share a common history of Afro-slavery, although with different processes of emancipation, laws and so forth. And even if though paths to emancipation were different in both countries—racial segregation versus racial miscegenation—the racist legacy of slavery and its ties to class and social inequalities and mobility are similar. Interestingly, even with their different geopolitical locations and interests and an obvious "asymmetrical flow of information" (Straubhaar, 1991) we can still trace similar patterns of representation between Brazilian and American media. Colonialism is also a common denominator, and the fact that in the fictional world of *Segundo Sol* two brothers were divided based on their *perceived* race clearly shows Brazil's colonial roots and the imposition of Eurocentric think-ing and values in Brazilian media and society (Martins et al, 2018, p. 140).

This points to another outcome of my research: it also offers a glimpse into the current racial zeitgeist in Brazil, including both changes and continuities in racial discourse over the past decade. For example, in 2008, *Duas Caras* was a breakthrough production that presented audiences with the first Black protagonist in a telenovela. In *Segundo Sol* a decade later, the existence of Blacks in Brazil was near eradicated, despite the show being set in Bahia. These facts of course reflected the wider sociopolitical atmospheres at the time of each production: over the decade, Brazil transitioned from a progres-sive to a populist conservative government. Even more fascinating was the public's reaction, involvement, and activism that resulted from that initial trailer for *Segundo Sol* and its erasure of Blacks in the initial stage of the production, which ultimately changed the path of the telenovela. This is a strikingly example of how telenovelas—whether in preproduction, during, or postproduction—contribute to a lively discussion about race in contemporary Brazil.

***

It was important to start this analysis with an overview of Brazilian history, especially the country's racial history, which includes notions of whitening and miscegenation. It was likewise important to begin by contextualizing my study within contemporary politics and racial politics, most significantly the shift from a progressive government to a more conservative one over the past decade. In addition to these broader contexts, I also situated my analysis of *Segundo Sol* by explaining the importance of TV Globo and its telenovelas not only in Brazil, but globally as well.

The introduction of this book also contained an explanation of my methodology, which I situated within a Cultural Studies tradition and a specifically Latin American Tradition, which helped me articulate TV audiences ultimately become "active-ists." In the Latin American context, as stated by Martín Barbero, one of the pioneers in the reconfiguration of media reception studies, many scholars have aligned with the Critical tradition to consider subjects as accomplices of domination, when they should in fact be considered as decoders and sometimes replicators of the domination discourses. In other words, in the reception space there is room for domination and, at the same time, for resistance and re-signification (Scolari, 2015, p. 1096). Drawing from the broader Cultural Studies tradition, we can employ Hall's encoding/decoding circuit to understand this relationship, which is the approach I took. Thus, the introduction and the first chapter were key to laying the groundwork for the textual analysis that followed.

In the body chapters of the book, I offered a careful analysis of Blacks and Blackness through exploring some key characters and their narrative arcs, in addition to other expressions of Blackness, such as its manifestation candomblé and capoeira. This analysis offered a glimpse into the role that telenovelas and various social actors play in constructing and disseminating ideas about race, racism, and social change. While *Segundo Sol* initially garnered negative attention, mainly due to the sheer lack of Black Brazilians featured as cast members in the trailer, the entirety of my investigation showed that the myth of Brazilian racial democracy is still alive even through the reality of racial equality is far from being achieved. Telenovelas, I have argued, can help ignite change to reconcile this inconsistency, especially since their narratives can work as "agenda setters," offering opportunities for broader public debate about race and racism.

This ability of telenovelas to generate discussion and change discourse is true both in Brazil and abroad. As Straubhaar (2012) suggests, Brazilian telenovelas are as much a national as a transnational product, in that they have adapted their storylines to cater to not just a domestic economic market, but also a marketplace of ideas. So, in addition to its traditional strategy of using narratives to address local political and social issues, more and more, topics cover issues of multiculturalism, globalization, migration and diaspora, racism and others in a way that make them not only locally, but internationally relevant. Other scholars such as Hamburger (2005) have approached telenovelas through Newcomb & Hirsch's (2000) "cultural forum" lenses: namely, they understand that telenovela audiences take topics presented to them as legitimate topics for public discussion through which they engage their personal experiences in public terms, that is, in terms that are recognized as legitimate by fellow viewers (p. 145). As we have seen, in a digital world, this is aided and exacerbated by turning viewers into not only creators of content, but into activists who are able to effect real change.

Thus, the representation of race and discussions about race and racism ignited by telenovelas are important in the daily lives of many Brazilians. Telenovelas speak to the everyday lives and concerns of viewers in addition to satisfying their curiosity regarding the unfolding of the narrative (Motter, 2003, p. 22); at many TV stations, telenovela programming is as or even more important than the news. Because of the significance of the genre, the ways in which race and racism are presented and represented in daily transnational programs such as telenovelas deserve both academic and popular scrutiny.

By tracing the representation of Afro-Brazilians in telenovelas and focusing on characters such as Zefa, Roberval, Acácio, Pai Didico and Doralice, I have shown the constraints and possibilities for representation in the telenovela medium. I have also demonstrated the value of future research into the representation of other Afro-Brazilian actors/characters in upcoming telenovelas. An investigation into future manifestations of Blackness in telenovelas, such as more detailed work on Candomblé and capoeira, is also needed. As discussed above, while there may be problematic portrayals of race in telenovelas, the genre continues to be a vital medium in the battleground of discourses that form individual's identities, including their racial identities. In the twenty-first century, ideas about identity, citizenship and belonging, as well as a global market of goods and ideas, are inevitably connected to what is consumed through the media.

Brazilian telenovelas, and more specifically TV Globo telenovelas, with their global reach, reflect, articulate, and disseminate both ingrained but also novel ideologies about race. Thus, future textual analyses of the type presented here are imperative, even if shows include as few as five main Black characters, as in the case of *Segundo Sol*. As a reminder, textual analysis looks for the struggle over meaning, and the presence of Black bodies and Black stories in telenovelas is not a mere struggle for numbers and data, but an active fight for the insertion of Black people and culture in the political, social and economic spheres. And while textual analysis tends to have a subjective character, due to the polysemic nature of texts, it is an important corrective to strictly quantitative analysis, which would "count the number of Black bodies," for example, on a given program. The nature of representation is just as important as how many are represented.

What is the role of telenovelas in society? How can they contribute to a critical public debate about race, racism, and political and social change? How can we demand multiple representations of realities that do not humiliate certain groups, or perpetuate longstanding stereotypes? What are the multiple readings that can be derived from telenovelas, and what types of reaction and or activism do they ignite? How can a melodramatic, traditional program such as a telenovela simultaneously serve as a catalyst for social change? These are questions that researchers should continue to pursue. Until then, I will "stay tuned, and stay active," and hope you will too.

NOTES

1. For example, according to a study, in 2017 investments in TV advertising were R\$ 26.9 billion. This was followed by online advertising (R\$ 11.7 billion), print advertising (R\$ 3.1 billion), billboard advertising (R\$ 1.5 billion), and radio advertising (R\$ 1.3 billion). According to research titled "State of Ad Tech 2019," Brazil is unique case in having such a high proportion of advertising expenditures directed toward television: globally, advertisers spend about 20 percent of their budgets on social media, 13 percent on paid displays, and 12 percent on TV, press, and radio combined (Navarro, 2019, para 1).

References

Adorno, T. W., & Horkheimer, M. 2002. *Dialectic of enlightenment.* Stanford, CA: Stanford University Press.

Anderson, M., Toor, S., Rainie, L., & Smith, A. 2018. Activism in the social media age: An Analysis of #BlackLivesMatter and other Twitter hashtags related to political or social issues. August 28. Pewresearch.org. https://www.pewresearch.org/internet/2018/07/11/an-analysis-of-blacklivesmatter-and-other-twitter-hashtags-related-to-political-or-social-issues/

Andrade, R. M. B. 2000. *O fim do mundo: O imaginário e teledramaturgia.* São Paulo, SP: Annablume.

Andrew, S. 2020. People are tweeting about Black Lives Matter now more than at any point in the movement's history. June 11. Cnn.com. https://edition.cnn.com/2020/06/11/us/black-lives-matter-hashtag-popularity-trnd/index.html

Andrews, G. R. 1991. *Blacks & whites in São Paulo, Brazil: 1888–1988.* Madison, WI: University of Wisconsin Press.

Após críticas à Bahia branca da Globo. 2018. '2º Sol' tem um negro para cada nova participação. September 05. Folha.uol.com.br. https://telepadi.folha.uol.com.br/apos-criticas-bahia-branca-2o-sol-tem-um-negro-para-cada-participacao/

Após críticas por falta de negros. 2018. Globo diz que não seleciona atores por cor de pele. May 03. Br.noticias.yahoo.com.br. https://br.noticias.yahoo.com/ap%C3%B3s-cr%C3%ADticas-por-falta-negros-212500678.html?guccounter=1

Após críticas por 'novela branca.' 2019. Globo fará especial de fim de ano só com baianos. April 15. https://www.uol.com.br. https://noticiasdatv.uol.com.br/noticia/televisao/apos-criticas-por-novela-branca-globo-fara-especial-de-fim-do-ano-so-com-baianos-26008?cpid=txt

Araújo, J. Z. 2000. *A negação do Brasil: O negro na telenovela brasileira.* São Paulo, SP: Senac.

Araújo, J. Z. 2008. O negro na dramaturgia. Um caso exemplar da decadência do mito da democracia racial brasileira. *Estudos Feministas, Florianópolis, 16(3): 424*, pp. 979–985.

Atores da Globo se reúnem e questionam falta de negros em novela. 2018, May 04. *Noticiasaominuto.com.br.* Retrieved March 10, 2020, from https://www

.noticiasaominuto.com.br/fama/586421/atores-da-globo-se-reunem-e-questionam-falta-de-negros-em-novela

Atrizes negras francesas vão denunciar em Cannes falta de representatividade no cinema. 2018, May 05. Uol.com.br. https://noticias.uol.com.br/ultimas-noticias/rfi/2018/05/04/atrizes-negras-francesas-vao-denunciar-em-cannes-falta-de-representatividade-no-cinema.htm

Azevedo, R. 2020. Raça Não Existe! August 1. Veja.com.br. https://veja.abril.com.br/blog/reinaldo/veja-4-materia-de-capa-raca-nao-existe/

Barros, M. 2018a. Fabrício Boliveira, de 'Segundo Sol': 'Faltam papéis centrais para negros.' Veja.com.br. June 20. Retrieved March 30, 2020, from https://veja.abril.com.br/cultura/fabricio-boliveira-de-segundo-sol-faltam-papeis-centrais-para-negros/

Barros, M. 2018b. Os acertos e erros de 'Segundo Sol.' November 9. Veja.com.br. Retrieved March 30, 2020, from https://veja.abril.com.br/entretenimento/os-acertos-e-erros-de-segundo-sol/

Benício, J. 2018. Globo racista? Trama De Roberval Poderá calar os críticos. May 22. *Terra.com.br.* https://www.terra.com.br/diversao/tv/blog-sala-de-tv/globo-racista-trama-de-roberval-podera-calar-os-criticos,8cb9b5e0faafb1592e48e149c8840e0caqh5dnnp.html

Bogle, D. 2001. *Toms, coons, mulattoes, mammies and bucks: An interpretive history of blacks in American films.* New York: Continuum.

Boylorn, R. M. 2008. As seen on TV: An autoethnographic reflection on race and reality television. *Critical Studies in Media Communication, 25(4)*, pp. 413–433.

Brazil profile—Timeline. 2019, January 03. *Bbc.com.* Retrieved February 1, 2020, from https://www.bbc.com/news/world-latin-america-19359111

Brazil's New Racist President Has Anti-Black Agenda. 2019, May 02. *Newsone.com.* Retrieved February 1, 2020, from https://newsone.com/3834167/jair-bolsonaro-brazil-president-affirmative-action-black-prople/

Caldwell, K. 2007. *Negras in Brazil: Re-envisioning black women, citizenship, and the politics of identity.* New Brunswick, NJ: Rutgers University Press.

Campos, L. A., Candido, M. R., & Feres, J. J. 2014. A Raça e o Gênero nas Novelas dos Últimos 20 Anos. Grupo de Estudos Multidisciplinares da Ação Afirmativa. Retrieved March 10, 2020, from http://gemaa.iesp.uerj.br/infografico/infografico3/

Carneiro, E. 2008. O candomblé na Bahia. São Paulo: Martins Fontes.

Carneiro, J. E. (Writer), & Carvalho, D., & De Médicis, M. (Directors). 2018, May 14. *Segundo Sol* [Television series]. Salvador, Bahia: Rede Globo.

Castro, D., & Guaraldo, L. 2017. Novos tempos: Globo troca atriz branca por negra em próxima novela. December 15. Uol.com.br. https://noticiasdatv.uol.com.br/noticia/novelas/novos-tempos-globo-troca-atriz-branca-por-negra-em-proxima-novela---18235?cpid=txt

Cena de 'Segundo Sol' gera polêmica entre religiosos. 2018, September 11. iBahia.com. https://www.ibahia.com/detalhe/noticia/cena-de-segundo-sol-gera-polemica-entre-religiosos/

Cena de 'Segundo Sol' sobre candomblé revolta internautas. 2018, September 11. Gente.ig.com.br. https://gente.ig.com.br/tvenovela/2018-09-11/segundo-sol-exu.html

Chefão da Globo. 2018. Schroder nega falta de investimento em negros. May 15. Uol.com.br. https://telepadi.folha.uol.com.br/chefao-da-globo-nega-falta-de-investimento-em-negros-e-sustenta-busca-por-representar-sociedade/

Collins, P. H. 2000. *Black Feminist Thought: Knowledge, Conscious and the Politics of Empowerment.* New York: Routledge.

Cowie, S. 2018. Bahia is Brazil's blackest state—but you'd never guess it from latest TV soap. May 18. Retrieved February 2, 2020, from https://www.theguardian.com/world/2018/may/18/brazil-segundo-sol-telenovela-White-black-cast-race

Da Silva, M. G. 2017. Negras! Somos Todas Maju: Um estudo sobre representação e racismo no jornal nacional, pp. 1–58. January 1. Lume.ufrgs.br. https://lume.ufrgs.br/handle/10183/177694

Daniel, G. R. 2006. *Race and multiraciality in Brazil and the United Sates. Converging paths?* University Park, PA: The Pennsylvania State University Press.

Dávila, A. M. 2001. *Latinos, Inc: The marketing and making of a people.* Berkeley, CA: University of California Press.

Depois da Globo. 2018. MP cobra representação racial de SBT e Record. June 07. Veja.abriu.com.br. https://veja.abril.com.br/cultura/depois-da-globo-mp-cobra-representacao-racial-de-sbt-e-record/

Dilma Diz que 'pobreza no Brasil Tem face negra e feminina.' 2011, November 19. Globo.com. http://g1.globo.com/economia/noticia/2011/11/dilma-diz-que-pobreza-no-brasil-tem-face-negra-e-feminina.html

Dos Santos, F. 2016. Câmera substitui Domingos Montagner em "Velho Chico" e comove internautas. September 27. Otvfoce.com.br. https://www.otvfoco.com.br/camera-substitui-domingos-montagner-em-velho-chico-e-comove-internautas/

Farias, C. 2018a. *Em "Segundo Sol," personagem de pai de santo desaparece da trama.* August 17. Uol.com.br. https://tvefamosos.uol.com.br/noticias/redacao/2018/08/17/em-segundo-sol-personagem-de-pai-de-santo-desaparece-da-trama.htm

Farias, C. 2018b. *"Minha esperança é que respeitem," diz ator sobre Candomblé em Segundo Sol.* June 1. Uol.com.br. https://tvefamosos.uol.com.br/noticias/redacao/2018/06/01/atores-de-segundo-sol-esperam-que-trama-quebre-tabus-sobre-o-candomble.htm

Fox, E. 1997. Media and Culture in Latin America. *In J. Corner, P. Schelsinger & R. Silverstone (Eds.), International Media Research: A Critical Survey.* New York: Routlege, pp. 184–295.

Fuller, L. 2001. Are we seeing things?: The pinesol lady and the ghost of aunt Jemima. *Journal of Black Studies, 32(1),* pp. 120–131.

García Canclini, N. 2001. *Consumers and citizens: Globalization and multicultural conflicts.* Minneapolis, MN: University of Minnesota Press.

Gillam, R. 2019. Book Review: The Color of Love: Racial Features, Stigma, and Socialization in Black Brazilian Families by Elizabeth Hordge-Freeman. *Feminist Review,* 121 (1), 94–95.

Gilliam, A., & Gilliam, O. 1995. Negociando a subjetividade da mulata no Brasil. *Estudos Feministas, 3*(2), 2nd ser., 525–543.

Gray, H. 1995. *Watching race: Television and the struggle for blackness.* Minneapolis, MN: The University of Minnesota Press.

Grijó, W. P., & Sousa, A. H. 2012. O negro na telenovela brasileira: A atualidade das representações. *Estudos Em Comunicação 11,* 185–204.

Guaraldo, L. 2018. *Líderes da umbanda criticam Segundo Sol: 'Ofende nossa religião.'* September 12. Noticiasdatv.uol.com.br. https://noticiasdatv.uol.com.br /noticia/novelas/lideres-da-umbanda-criticam-segundo-sol-ofende-nossa-religiao --22292?cpid=txt

Hall, S. 1993. *Encoding, decoding. In: During, S. (Editor), The cultural studies reader.* New York: Routledge. p. 507–517.

Hall, S. 1995. The White of Their Eyes: Racist Ideologies and Media. In 1 G. Dines & J. M. Humez (Ed.), *Gender, race, and class in media: A critical reader.* Thousand Oaks, CA: Sage Publications.

Hall, S. 2006. *A identidade cultural na pós-modernidade.* Rio de Janeiro (RJ): DP & A.

Hamburger, E. 1998. Diluindo fronteiras: A televisão e as novelas no cotidiano. In L. M. Schwarcz (Ed.), História da vida privada no Brasil: *Contrastes da intimidade contemporânea* (Vol. 4, pp. 439–489). São Paulo: Companhia das Letras.

Hamburger, E. 2005. *O Brasil antenado: A sociedade na novela.* Rio de Janeiro: Zahar.

Hooks, B. 1992. *Black locks: Race and representation.* Boston, MA: South End Press.

Hordge-Freeman, E. 2015. *The Color of Love: Racial Features, Stigma, and Socialization in Black Brazilian Families.* Austin: University of Texas Press.

Ito, C. 2017. Negro drama. Ser homem negro no Brasil é conviver com uma série de estereótipos, que envolvem gênero, raça e classe social. Discutir isso é reiterar a noção básica de que ninguém é uma coisa só. *Revistatrip.uol.com.br.* https://revistatrip.uol.com.br/trip/masculinidade-negra-ser-homem-negro-no-brasil -e-conviver-com-uma-serie-de-estereotipos-que-envolvem-genero-raca-e-classe -social

Jenkins, H. 2004. The Cultural Logic of Media Convergence. *International Journal of Cultural Studies, 7*(1), 33–43.

Jenkins, H. 2006. *Convergence culture: Where old and new media collide.* New York: New York University Press.

Joyce, S. N. 2012. *Brazilian telenovelas and the myth of racial democracy.* Lanham, MD: Lexington Books.

Joyce, S. N. 2013. A kiss is (not) just a kiss: Heterodeterminism, homosexuality, and TV Globo telenovelas. *International Journal of Communication, 7*(1), 48–66.

Joyce, S. N. 2020. Thriving telenovelas: TV Globo's strategies for keeping the genre relevant, Popular Communication, DOI: 10.1080/15405702.2020.1841198

Joyce, S. N., & LaPastina, A. 2017. Women and criminality in Brazilian telenovelas: Salve Jorge and human trafficking. In M. Buonanno (Ed.), *Television antiheroines: Women behaving badly in crime and prison drama* (pp. 219–235). Bristol, UK: Intellect.

Joyce, S. N., & LaPastina, A. 2019. Subjective camera, direct address, and audience participation. Velho Chico and a new Brazilian telenovela aesthetics (pp.39–46). In Sigismondi, P. (Editor), *World entertainment media: Global, regional, and local perspectives.* New York: Routledge.

Joyce, S. N., & Martinez, M. 2016. BRICS and mediated narratives: The proximity between Brazilian news and telenovelas. *Brazilian Journalism Review, 12(1)*, 82–101.

Joyce, S. N., & Martinez, M. 2017. *From Social Merchandising to Social Spectacle: Portrayals of Domestic Violence in TV Globo's Prime-Time Telenovelas.* International Journal of Communication 11, 220–236. https://ijoc.org/index.php/ijoc/article/view/5905/1894

Joyce, S. N., & Martinez, M. 2019a. "The Talk," and the one who shall not be named: A case study on racial and gender discourses on NBC's *Parenthood. Revista Eco-Pós.* https://revistaecopos.eco.ufrj.br/eco_pos/article/view/13

Joyce, S. N, & Martinez, M. 2019b. A "conversa" e "aquele que não deve ser nomeado": Um estudo de caso sobre a série americana Parenthood sobre discurso e representações raciais e de gênero "The Talk," and the one who shall not be named: A case study on racial and gender discourses on NBC's *Parenthood. Revista ECO-Pós, 22*(2), 270–292.

Júnior, A. 2018. Internet critica Segundo Sol por representar uma Bahia branca e lança campanha "Eu poderia estar na novela." April 30. Otvfoco.com.br. https://www.otvfoco.com.br/internet-critica-segundo-sol-por-representar-uma-bahia-branca-e-lanca-campanha-eu-poderia-estar-na-novela/

Kaiser, A. J. 2019. 'It's our problem': Brazilian drama brings Amazon rainforest battle to screen. Theguardian.com. Retrieved from https://www.theguardian.com/tv-and-radio/2019/jul/13/arua nas-brazil-amazon-rainforest-drama-marcos-nisti

Leahy, J., & Schipani, A. 2018. Soap opera row shines light on treatment of black Brazilians. June 18. *FinancialTimes.com.* Retrieved February 19, 2020, from https://www.ft.com/content/e5700466-7076-11e8-92d3-6c13e5c92914

Lobo, N. & Orofino, M. I. 2008. *Duas Faces de Duas Caras: Por um enfoque "prismático" do comentário social na telenovela.* [Conference Paper]. Intercom—Sociedade Brasileira de Estudos Interdisciplinares da Comunicação. Presented at XXXI Congresso Brasileiro de Ciências da Comunicação. Natal: RN. [Electronic Version]. http://74.125.95.132/search?q=cache:RLizd_mz0HYJ:intercom.org.br/papers/nacionais/2008/resumos/R3-1539 1.pdf+duas+caras,+racismo&cd=50&hl=en&ct=clnk&gl=us

Lopes, M. I. V., & Gómez, G. O. 2017. Ibero-American observatory of television fiction obitel 2017. One decade of television fiction in Ibero-America: An analysis of ten years of Obitel (2007–2016). Retrieved 2020, from http://www.obitel.net/wp-content/uploads/2017/09/obitel-2017-ingles.pdf

Lopes, M. I. V. & Greco, C. Brasil 2018. Dinâmicas da ficção televisiva na transição multicanal. In: Lopes, M. I. V. & Gomes, G. O. (Eds.). *Ficção televisiva ibero americana em plataformas de video on demand.* Porto Alegre: Sulina, pp. 103–128.

Lopes, M. I. V., Borelli, S. H. S., & Resende, V. da R. 2002. *Vivendo com a telenovela: mediações, recepção, teleficcionalidade.* São Paulo: Summus Editorial.

Lopes, M. I., Gómez, G. O., & Lopes, M. I. 2015. *Relações de gênero na ficção televisiva: Obitel 2015.* Porto Alegre: Sulina.

Machado, G. 2018. O "segundo sol" não vai chegar: Os personagens apagados na novela das 21h. November 6. *Uol.com.br.* https://tvefamosos.uol.com.br/listas/o-segundo-sol-nao-vai-chegar-os-personagens-apagados-na-novela-das-21h.htm

Maranhão, R. 2009. Com reforço de Lula, 'seleção' brasileira usa a emoção na cartada final por 2016. Globoesporte.globo.com. Retrieved from http://globoesporte.globo.com/Esportes/Noticias/Olimpiadas/0,,MUL1326806-17698,00-COM+REFORCO+DE+LULA+SELECAO+BRASILEIRA+USA+A+EMOCAO+NA+CARTADA+FINAL+POR.html

Martín-Barbero, J. 1993. *Communication, culture and hegemony: From media to mediations.* London/Newbury Park: Sage.

Martín-Barbero, J. 2001. *Dos meios às mediações: Comunicação, cultura e hegemonia [From media to mediations: Communication, culture and hegemony].* Rio de Janeiro, Brazil: UFRJ.

Martín-Barbero, J., & Muñoz, S. 1992. *Televisión y melodrama: Géneros y lecturas de la telenovela en Colombia.* Bogotá, Colombia: Tercer Mundo.

Martins, Z., Raika, J., Basthi, A., Moura, A., & Azevedo, L. M. 2018. Do racismo epistêmico às cotas raciais: A demanda por abertura na universidade. *Revistas.ufrj.br.* https://revistas.ufrj.br/index.php/eco_pos/article/view/20276

Mitchell, J. 2020. *Imagining the mullatta. Blackness in U.S. and Brazilian Media.* Urbana: University of Illinois Press.

Motter, M. L. 2003. *Ficção e realidade: A construção do cotidiano na telenovela.* Comunicação ed. São Paulo, SP: Alexa Cultural.

Mulvey, L. 1999. *Visual pleasure and narrative cinema.* Screen 16(4), pp.6–18.

Não vão deixar saudades! Veja quem são os piores personagens de "Segundo Sol." (2018, October 25). Gente.ig.com.br https://gente.ig.com.br/tvenovela/2018-10-26/piores-personagens-segundo-sol.html

Nascentes, Z. C. 2017. *Nem cruz nem encruzilhada: diversidade religiosa em Amor à vida, TV Globo / Neither cross nor crossroads: religious diversity in Amor à vida, Globo TV.* PLURA, Revista de Estudos de Religião / PLURA, Journal for the Study of Religion. https://revistaplura.emnuvens.com.br/plura/article/view/1306

Navarro, V. 2019. TV segue como principal investimento do marketing brasileiro. *meioemensagem.com.br.* https://www.meioemensagem.com.br/home/midia/2019/04/09/tv-segue-como-principal-investimento-do-marketing-brasileiro.html

Newcomb, H. & Hirsch, P. M. 2000. Television as cultural forum. In H. Newcomb (Eds.) *Televison: The critical view* (6th edition). New York: Oxford University Press.

Novela 'Segundo Sol': Acácio transa com Renatinha e Ludi ao mesmo tempo. 2018, August 07. *Purepeople.com.br.* https://www.purepeople.com.br/noticia/novela-segundo-sol-acacio-tem-sexo-a-tres-apos-manuela-pedir-para-reatar-namoro_a237424/1

Nunes, J. L. N., Araujo, L. K., Serejo, L. A. F., Vieira, L. M., Cutrim, L. G. B., & Sena, P. R. C. 2019. 18 anos de história: A falsa democracia racial e a presença do negro como protagonistas nas novelas das 8 e 9 da Rede Globo de 2000 a 2018.

Portalintercom.org.br. https://portalintercom.org.br/anais/nordeste2019/resumos/ R67-0397-1.pdf

Page, J. 1995. *The Brazilians*. New York: Addison-Wesley.

Pelo fim da violência contra a juventude negra no Brasil. 2018. *Nacoesunidas.org*. Retrieved January 7, 2020, from https://nacoesunidas.org/campanha/vidas-negras/ Pelo fim da violência contra a juventude negra no Brasil. (2018). *Nacoesunidas.org*. Retrieved January 7, 2020, from https://nacoesunidas.org/campanha/vidas-negras/ mar

Pereira Jr., A. 2012. Acerto de cotas. Folha de São Paulo. https://www1.folha.uol .com.br/paywall/login.shtml?https%3A%2F%2Fwww1.folha.uol.com.br%2Ffsp %2Filustrada%2F73055-acerto-de-cotas.shtml

Pereira, M. 2018. Em Segundo Sol, Roberval é humilhado pelo pai racista: 'Negrinho bastardo e sujo.' July 2. *Noticiasdatv.uol.com.br*. https://noticiasdatv.uol.com.br /noticia/novelas/em-segundo-sol-roberval-e-humilhado-pelo-pai-racista-negrinho -bastardo-e-sujo--21143

Phillips, T. 2020Jair Bolsonaro's racist comment sparks outrage from indigenous groups. January 24. *Theguardian.com*. Retrieved February 1, 2020, from https: //www.theguardian.com/world/2020/jan/24/jair-bolsonaro-racist-comment-sparks -outrage-indigenous-groups

Port, M. V. 2006. Visualizing the sacred: Video technology, "televisual" style, and the religious imagination in Bahian candomblé. *American Ethnologist, 33*(3), 444–461.

Potascheff, A. 2019. 'Falta subjetividade negra na ficção.' *Revistatrip.uol.com.br*. https://revistatrip.uol.com.br/trip-fm/fabricio-boliveira-fala-sobre-roberval -segundo-sol-wilson-simonal-racismo-e-representatividade

Ramos, A. 2003. O negro no Brasil. Rio de Janeiro: Graphia

Rêgo, C. M. 2009. Beyond Globo. Journal of International Communication, 15(1), 37–55. doi:10.1080/13216597.2009.9674743

Rêgo, C. M. 2011. From humble beginnings to international prominence: The history and development of Brazilian telenovelas (pp. 75–92). In Rios, D. I. & Castañeda, M. (Editor), *Soap operas and telenovelas in the digital age*. New York: Peter Lang.

Ricco, S. 2019. Plano de novelas mais curtas já está implantado na Globo. January 29. Tvefamosos.com.br. https://tvefamosos.uol.com.br/colunas/flavio-ricco/2019/01 /29/plano-de-novelas-mais-curtas-ja-e-realidade-na-globo.htm?utm_campaign=ve -tv&utm_content=hyperlink-texto&utm_medium=email&utm_source=newsletter

Ríos, D. I., & Castañeda, M. (Eds.). 2011. *Soap operas and telenovelas in the digital age: Global industries and new audiences*. New York: Peter Lang.

Rochelle tenta conquistar Acácio: 'Você é lindo e eu sou maravilhosa.' 2018, July 1. *Jornaldamidia.com.br*. https://www.jornaldamidia.com.br/2018/07/01/segundo-sol -rochelle-tenta-conquistar-acacio-voce-e-lindo-e-eu-sou-maravilhosa/

Rodrigues, G. 2018. Segundo Sol: Rochelle tem noite quente com Acácio e depois pede foto: "É tendência." July 2. *Observatoriodatv.uol.com.br*. https://observatoriodatv .uol.com.br/noticias/2018/07/segundo-sol-rochelle-tem-noite-quente-com-acacio-e -depois-pede-foto-e-tendencia

Santana, G. 2018. "O Roberval é traumatizado," analisa Fabrício Boliveira sobre seu personagem em Segundo Sol. August 11. *Observatoriodatv.uol.com.br*. https://

observatoriodatv.uol.com.br/entrevista/o-roberval-e-traumatizado-analisa-fabricio
-boliveira-sobre-seu-personagem-em-segundo-sol

Santos, G. A. 2002. *A invenção do ser negro: Um percurso das idéias que natural-
izam a inferioridade dos negros.* São Paulo: Educ/Fapesp; Rio de Janeiro: Pallas.

Santos, I. A. A. 2015. *Direitos humanos e as práticas de racismo.* Brasília: Edição
Câmara dos Deputados, Centro de Documentação e Informação.

Scolari, C. A. 2015. From (new)media to (hyper)mediations. Recovering Jesús
Martín-Barbero's mediation theory in the age of digital communication and cultural convergence. *Information, Communication & Society, 18*(9), 1092–1107. doi
:10.1080/1369118x.2015.1018299

'Segundo Sol': Ausência de negros em novela motiva movimento. 2018, May
5. Catracalivre.com.br. https://catracalivre.com.br/cidadania/ausencia-negros-o
-segundo-sol-samara-felippo/

'Segundo Sol' causa polêmica com cena sobre candomblé e gera revolta na internet.
2020, May 5. Catracalivre.com.br. https://catracalivre.com.br/cidadania/segundo
-sol-polemiza-com-cena-sobre-candomble-e-gera-revolta/

'Segundo Sol' é criticada por mostrar uma 'Bahia branca demais.' 2018, May
22. Catracalivre.com.br. https://catracalivre.com.br/cidadania/segundo-sol-bahia
-branca/

Shah, S., & Widjaya, R. 2020. Posts mentioning 'Black lives matter' spiked on lawmakers' social media accounts after George Floyd killing. August 20. Pewresearch.org.
https://www.pewresearch.org/fact-tank/2020/07/16/posts-mentioning-black-lives
-matter-spiked-on-lawmakers-social-media-accounts-after-george-floyd-killing/

Soares, M. A. D. S. 2012. Look, blackness in Brazil: Disrupting the grotesquerie of
racial representation in Brazilian visual culture. *Cultural Dynamics, 24*(1), 75–101.

Sovik, L. 2009. *Aqui ninguém é branco.* Rio de Janeiro, RJ: Aeroplano.

Straubhaar, J. D. 1991. Beyond media imperialism: Asymmetrical interdependence
and cultural proximity. Critical Studies in Mass Communication, 8(1), 39–59.
doi:10.1080/15295039109366779

Straubhaar, J. D. 2012. Telenovelas in Brazil: From travelling scripts to a genre and
proto-format both national and transnational. In: Orent, T. & Shahaf, S. (Eds.).
In *Global television formats: Understanding television across borders.* New York:
Routledge, 2012. pp. 148–177.

Stycer, M. 2018. Elenco questiona falta de negros em "Segundo Sol" e Globo promete
"evoluir." Uol.com.br. https://mauriciostycer.blogosfera.uol.com.br/2018/05/03/
elenco-questiona-falta-de-negros-em-segundo-sol-e-globo-promete-evoluir/

Terto, A. 2018. "Segundo Sol": A Bahia branca da novela é bem diferente da
Bahia real, com 76% de negro. Huffpostbrasil.com. Retrieved March 10, 2020,
from https://www.huffpostbrasil.com/2018/04/30/a-ausencia-de-atores-negros-em
-segundo-sol-novela-da-globo-ambientada-na-bahia_a_23424010/

Travae, M. 2018a. "It's not religious intolerance and is indeed racism," says bàbá during roundtable on violence against the sacred spaces of African-oriented religions
like Candomblé. December 12. Blackwomenofbrazil.com. https://blackbraziltoday
.com/its-not-religious-intolerance/

Travae, M. 2018b. Rede Globo TV sued for low percentage of Black actors in novela set in state of Bahia; state nearly 80% Black but main cast of soap opera is nearly 90% white. May 15. *Blackwomenofbrazil.com*. https://blackwomenofbrazil.co/rede -globo-tv-sued-for-low-percentage-of-black-actors/

Travae, M. 2020. Orisha statue is a target of vandalism in in Salvador, Bahia; a symbol of deities, it is the latest violent assault on African religious symbols. October 22. Blackwomenofbrazil.com. https://blackbraziltoday.com/orisha-statue -is-a-target-of-vandalism-in-salvador-bahia/

Vanicléia Santos: "O patuá nasce de recriações da cultura negra na diáspora." (n.d.). http://blogs.correio24horas.com.br/emcantos/vanicleia-santos-o-patua -nasce-de-recriacoes-da-cultura-negra-na-diaspora/

Vieira, R. 2018a. Segundo Sol: Conheça Acácio, o Personagem capoeirista Da nova novela das 21h. May 16. *Observatoriodatv.uol.com.br.* https://observatoriodatv.uol .com.br/noticias/2018/05/conheca-acacio-o-personagem-negro-e-capoeirista-de -segundo-sol-nova-novela-das-21h

Vieira, R. 2018b. *Conheça Groa, o personagem gringo de Segundo Sol, nova novela das 21h.* May 16. Segundo Sol: Conheça Groa, o personagem gringo da novela. Observatoriodatv.uol.com.br. https://observatoriodatv.uol.com.br/noticias/conheca -groa-o-personagem-gringo-de-segundo-sol-nova-novela-das-21h

Voeks, R. A. 2003. *Sacred leaves of Candomblé: African magic, medicine, and religion in Brazil.* Austin: University of Texas Press.

Index

Acácio, 45, 53–54, 56, 58–66, 68, 70
Acaiabe, João, 80–82.
  See also Pai Didico
active, 4, 19, 20, 22, 25, 26–27, 30, 31,
  63, 68, 69, 82, 90.
  See also activism; encoding/
    decoding; Hall, Stuart
activism, 19.
  See also encoding/decoding,
    Hall, Stuart
active-ists, 2, 24, 25, 27–31, 82, 91, 93.
  See also activism
Adorno, Theodor, 21
affirmative action, 3, 11, 16n1,
  36, 38, 49;
  quotas, 3
Afro-Brazilian, 1, 10–12, 16n1, 28, 33,
  35–37, 39, 41, 43, 48, 54, 66, 73, 77,
  78, 81–87, 90, 92
agenda setter, 4, 21, 91
Aldeia Caboclo Flecheiro, 83
Anderson, Monica, 26
Andrew, Scottie, 43
Araújo, Joel Zitto, 5, 6–7, 10, 33, 34
Araújo, Taís, 36.
  See also Helena
Ariella, 75
Athayde, Claudine, 37, 38–42, 49

Athayde, Severo, 41, 42–45, 49, 51n1,
  53, 57, 60, 62, 66, 67, 68, 70
Axé, 74, 88n2
Azevedo, Reinaldo, 45

Babylônia, 37
Bahia, 1, 4–5, 27, 29–31, 33, 54,
  55, 56, 59, 67, 73, 74, 75, 78, 81,
  85, 88n2, 90
Bantu, 73, 82
Barros, Mabi, 5, 54, 58, 68
Benício, Jeff, 55, 57, 70
Biju, Andréia, 73, 76, 87.
  See also Candomblé; Doralice; *Duas*
    Caras; Pai Didico; *terreiro*
Black movement, 2, 54, 58
Blackness, 34, 55, 73, 74, 85, 86, 87,
  89, 91, 92
Bogle, Donald, 34, 46, 54
Boliveira, Fabrício, 44, 54–56,
  58, 68, 70.
  See also Roberval
Bolsonaro, Jair, 1, 11
Boylorn, Robin, 13, 34, 37
branqueamento, 3, 7
Brazilian Institute of Geography and
  Statistics (IBGE), 10

105

About the Author

Samantha Nogueira Joyce is associate professor of global communication at Saint Mary's College of California. She studies media history, theory, and criticism with concentrations in cultural studies, critical theory, critical race theory, Latin American and Brazilian media, and cultural studies. Her research covers a range of contemporary as well as historical topics in order to understand the many ways in which people's identities are constituted by and through the media, especially television. In addition to her book *Brazilian Telenovelas and the Myth of Racial Democracy,* her research has appeared in *Popular Communication, International Journal of Communication,* and *Brazilian Journalism Research,* and in books such as *Television Antiheroines: Women Behaving Badly in Crime and Prison Drama,* and *World Entertainment Media: Global, Regional and Local Perspectives.*

www.ingramcontent.com/pod-product-compliance
Lightning Source LLC
Chambersburg PA
CBHW022327280326
41932CB00010B/1252